Keep *the* Candle Burning

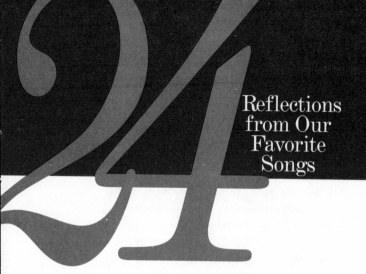

Reflections from Our Favorite Songs

Keep *the* Candle Burning

Point *of* Grace

WARNER
Faith

A Division of AOL Time Warner Book Group

Scripture quotations are taken from the
HOLY BIBLE: NEW INTERNATIONAL VERSION®.
Copyright © 1973, 1978, 1984 by International Bible Society.
Used by permission of Zondervan Publishing House.
All rights reserved.

WARNER *Faith*™ A Division of AOL Time Warner Book Group

Printed in the United States of America
First Warner Books printing: November 2003
10 9 8 7 6 5 4 3 2 1

Library of Congress Cataloging-in-Publication Data

Keep the candle burning : 24 reflections from our favorite songs /
Point of Grace.
p. cm.
ISBN 0-446-53134-0
1. Devotional literature, English.   2. Point of Grace (Musical group)
3. Contemporary Christian music—History and criticism.
I. Point of Grace (Musical group)
BV4832.3K44 2003
264'.23—dc21
2003057194

Book Design by Chris Welch

For John Mays
An exceptionally gifted visionary, mentor, friend
Who gave us a platform to share our hearts

Contents

✳

Acknowledgments

Point of Grace would like to thank our husbands, children, parents, and sisters for all of your support over the last twelve years. You are the reason we have made it this far! This unexpected musical journey we embarked on in college has been so much sweeter because of your love and devotion to us and this ministry.

We would also like to thank Bob DeMoss for capturing our voice on paper like no one else ever has. You are incredible. You have made something beautiful from a few small nuggets of our lives. We know people will be blessed and changed by this book. We are amazed at your talent.

Finally, to quote a line from one of the earliest songs we ever recorded, "Without the love of Jesus, tell me where would we be? Thank you,

✳

Lord, for where we are because of your great love for us.

Shelley, Denise, Heather, Terry

May 2003

Introduction

There's an interesting exchange between Job and God in the Old Testament. Maybe you remember the story. Job had been blessed by God with riches, a large family, and thousands of sheep and cattle. As God would have it, one day and without warning, Job lost everything he owned.

In chapter two, we find the newly impoverished Job sitting on an ash heap scraping his disease-covered skin with a piece of broken pottery. As if he weren't in enough misery, Job's indignant wife urged Job to "Curse God and die!" (Job 2:9).

Worse, three of Job's closest friends sat next to him on the ash heap to heap on their own sour advice. Their bitter exchange dragged on for the better part of twenty-two chapters. Exhausted, weary, and tired of scratching his skin raw, Job cried out for vindication.

✳

That's when God spoke.

That's when God painted the big picture for Job.

That's when Job's perspective of God was radically and forever changed.

Each of us, like Job, is on a journey. God is at work behind the scenes and we don't always know what God is up to—or why he moves the way he moves. Sometimes he rains down his blessing. Other times hardship rules the day. Through it all, as Job learned, one thing remains unchanged: God is still God. He is very much in control. And his love for you and for us is unshakable, no matter what comes our way.

When we started to sing together twelve years ago, we were four college-aged kids with a love for the Lord and a song in our hearts. We never imagined God would bless our musical journey with twenty-four number one hits in a row. Praise be his name.

Jesus is, after all, why we sing.

Looking back on the Lord's endless blessings, we thought it would be appropriate to invite you to go deeper with us into these songs. There's a story and a lesson behind each one. Our prayer is that you will find yourself refreshed, encouraged, challenged, convicted, and, most importantly, drawn closer to the heart of Jesus as you reflect on these meditations.

✳

Maybe you are in a place in your life that seems like Job's situation. Maybe you're having a difficult time in school, in your marriage, in your job, or perhaps you're wrestling with some physical ailment. On the other hand, maybe you are basking in the rich blessings from the Father. No matter where you are, we invite you to spend some time with us as we pursue the heart of God.

✳

Keep *the* Candle Burning

I'll Be Believing

Denise Jones

A friend shared this story with me and assured me that it actually happened. I'm told a pastor was sitting in his home office preparing for the Sunday service. His backyard, an oversized lot with tall trees, provided an inspiring view as he worked. This particular afternoon, he happened to spot a kitten who had climbed up a thin maple. For several minutes, the kitten cried out, unable to make her way down to safety.

Maybe the pastor had decided he needed a sermon illustration. Maybe he got tired of the kitten's cry. Whatever his motivation, he put aside his studies, went to the kitchen, fetched a bowl of milk, and then attempted to coax the kitty down. He tried cooing, "Here, kitty-kitty." He even tried words of encouragement. Nothing worked. The poor, frightened creature clung to a scrawny branch for dear life.

With his hands on his hips, the pastor sized up the situation. The tree, he noted, was less than three inches thick. There was just no way he could heave himself up to rescue the cat. What about a ladder? After a minute, he figured it was too risky to lean a ladder against the spindly tree.

Frustrated at the time he was wasting on this interruption, he was tempted to give up. It was then that a sudden blast of inspiration hit him. What if he bent the tree downward? He could easily reach up and get the kitten.

But how would he bend it?

The pastor decided to tie an old rope to the tree and then attach the other end to the bumper of his car. I'm serious. He thought that by pulling the car slowly forward he would gently ease the maple into position for a quick rescue. Within minutes, everything was set. The car. The rope. The tree. The frightened kitten.

He slipped behind the steering wheel of his car and pulled forward several feet. He walked back and checked the distance. The cat was still too far to reach. He nudged the car forward again. Same results. He also noticed how taut the rope had

✳

become and was unsure whether or not to take another chance. But he had come this far, so what choice did he have? This time, he inched forward and you can probably guess what happened.

The rope snapped.

The tree jolted upright.

And kitty sailed through the air, landing out of sight.

Stunned, the pastor prayed, "Lord, I tried. I now commit that kitten into your keeping." Before heading back to his study to finish the sermon preparation, he knocked on several neighbors' doors. Had they seen a little lost kitty? No. It was as if the cat had evaporated into thin air.

Several days later, the pastor bumped into a member from his congregation, a woman who lived nearby. As they talked, he glanced at the items in her shopping cart and was shocked to see a bag of cat food. He was surprised because her dislike of cats was almost legendary. Curiosity got the better of him, so he asked what she was doing buying cat food.

She said, "Pastor, you won't believe this. My little girl has been begging me almost every day for a cat. Well, I can't stand the little creatures, as you know, so I told her, 'If God gives you a cat, you can keep it.'"

The pastor had an idea of where this was going.

Maybe you do, too.

The woman said, "My girl is a little powerhouse of faith. She just kept believing God would provide. You know what she did? She marched outside, got down on her knees and prayed to Jesus for a cat. You're not going to believe this. I saw it with my own eyes. A little tan and white kitten came flying out of the clear blue sky with its tiny paws outspread, landing at my daughter's side!"

Unbelievable? Like I said, I'm told it's a true story. Even if my friend were mistaken, it's a picture of how God works. Time after time he demonstrates he's not so distracted by the affairs of the universe that he is unable to hear the petitions of a child. What a fun example of how he sometimes chooses to answer our prayers in the most unusual ways.

I like what King David said in Psalm 37:4: "Delight yourself in the Lord and he will give you the desires of your heart." This little girl, knowing full well how much her mother opposed pets, patiently believed God would overcome the odds. She in her own way delighted in the Lord and his provision. He, in turn, came through with, um, flying colors.

Listen to this amazing promise in Deuteronomy 31:8: "The Lord himself goes before you and will be

✳

with you; he will never leave you nor forsake you. Do not be afraid; do not be discouraged."

Let that sink in. As the song says, "Out here on my own, I won't be alone." Why? Because the God of the heavens promises to never, ever leave us. He hears our prayers. He is not distracted. If anything, he is waiting for you and me with open arms to call on his name.

Has life thrown you a curve? Does it feel as if the bottom has dropped out? Do you find yourself struggling with loneliness? Discouragement? Despair? Then take heart. Keep believing, keep trusting, keep waiting on the one who loves to delight us with good things—when we make him the delight of our hearts.

And who knows? He may answer your prayers with something that lands in your lap out of the blue.

*

I n Psalm 37:4, King David reveals how we, like that little girl in the story, can experience the desires of our heart. What was his secret? What are the obstacles in your life that might prevent you from fully embracing David's secret?

_____

_____

_____

_____

_____

_____

_____

_____

_____

_____

_____

_____

_____

_____

_____

✳

One More Broken Heart
Shelley Breen

I've lost track of the number of cities and places we've visited as a band. After the first several hundred towns, life on the road becomes a blur. Truthfully, to sit on a plane or bus for hours at a time isn't what it's cracked up to be. Dorothy, in *The Wizard of Oz*, was right. "There's no place like home."

But one of the pluses I've always enjoyed about life on the road was to bump into the odd, offbeat little places on the map. Along the way, for instance, I've discovered there is a little town called Hell, Michigan. I'm not making this up.

Hell is located in the southeast part of the state, about midway between Lansing, the state capital, and Ann Arbor. It's not far from Angels Pass and Monks Road. And, as you might expect, the highway to Hell is paved with crass signs telling you where to go.

*

Hell even has its own weather station, general store, and post office. People from neighboring towns often go to Hell when mailing their taxes to the IRS or alimony payments to a former spouse. And tourists have this burning desire to send their friends a postcard from Hell. Me? I've got to wonder, who in their right mind would buy a house in, um, Hell?

How would you raise your children to take hell seriously?

All fun aside, the Bible teaches that hell is a very real place. Jesus described hell as a place "where the fire never goes out" (Mark 9:43b). He paints for us another picture of hell as a place of "torment" in the parable of the rich man and Lazarus (Luke 16:23). Jesus also describes this banishment from heaven as a place of "darkness, where there will be weeping and gnashing of teeth" (Matt. 8:12).

Really? Look at Mark 9:48. Jesus teaches us that hell is a place where "their worm does not die, and the fire is not quenched."

The good news is that those who embrace what Jesus has done on the cross will escape this fiery judgment. In Matthew 25, Jesus talks to his disciples about his return. He tells the story of the sheep and the goats, where the King welcomes the sheep into a

✳

"kingdom prepared for you since the creation of the world" (v. 34). Then the King will say to the goats, "Depart from me, you who are cursed, into the eternal fire prepared for the devil and his angels" (v. 41).

Probably one of the hardest things for me is to imagine the fact that hell is forever. Look at verse 46. Jesus says, "Then they will go away to eternal punishment, but the righteous to eternal life."

Does this talk about hell make you uncomfortable? I know it sure makes me squirm.

Then again, maybe that's a good thing. Maybe the severity of hell will light a fire under my lazy behind and rekindle a passion for those who are lost . . . those who will never know the love, the joy, the peace, and the majesty of Jesus . . . those who will spend their forever in torment.

Look at it this way. This is the only time in all of history when you and I have the privilege to share Christ with those who need salvation. Once the Lord comes back, it will be too late to urge our friends to run from death into life. There is no second chance. No back door. No escape hatch.

Sometimes I imagine that awesome day of judgment and shudder.

I think about the friends and acquaintances standing in line around me. Friends who are lost and who will one day be assigned their eternal destiny. My heart will most certainly be crushed to think that I didn't take the time to love them, to be Jesus to them, to give them the chance to avoid hell.

I also imagine them looking at me with puzzled faces, wondering why I cared so little. No wonder every time we sing this song, I stand convicted. Too often I let the dumb stuff of life get in the way. I spend far too much time watching television. I waste way too much time on petty junk that doesn't matter in the scope of eternity.

Maybe that's because I forget that sharing Jesus with a dying world isn't optional. He commands us to "Go into all the world and preach the good news to all creation" (Mark 16:15). As the song says, "Let me show them that You love them. Won't you help me bring them in?"

And the next time you're driving through Michigan, I know the perfect place to start!

✳

Keep *the* Candle Burning

*D*o you have any neighbors, friends, or family members who don't know the Lord? Why not jot down their names. Is the time spent viewing TV getting in the way of sharing your faith with them?

_____

_____

_____

_____

_____

_____

_____

_____

_____

_____

_____

_____

_____

_____

_____

✳

Jesus Will Still Be There

Heather Payne

When we started Point of Grace twelve years ago, we were four crazy college girls. But we were way more than members of a band. We were friends. Close friends. Very close friends. You see, Terry, Denise, and I had known each other ever since the fifth grade. We hooked up with Shelley in college. From then on we basically hung out, laughed, goofed off, and ultimately dreamed of sharing our faith in music together.

We were four inseparable friends.

Several years into this delightful sisterhood, the clouds rolled in. The rain came. And time stood still. We had been invaded. What had been a close circle was suddenly threatened by the infiltration of the Enemy.

Stu.

✳

Okay, so Denise's husband, Stu, is really a nice guy *now*. But then, he was The Outsider. I'm sure Denise probably felt a little guilty for falling in love with Stu while the rest of us were striking out on the guy scene. I wouldn't be surprised if Denise knew we were also concerned about the future plans for the band. I mean, in our view, once Denise was married, she might move away and leave us in the dust.

In fact, the first summer we were singing together as a group, a wise man told us, "As long as you are single, this singing thing will be great. But once husbands come along, forget about it. You career will be all over." With that thought ringing in our ears, the inevitable happened.

Denise and Stu got married.

So there we were, Shelley, Terry, and I, roommates living in a Nashville apartment, while Denise and Stu had their own place. We had our inside jokes of which Denise was no longer a part, and I'm sure she felt uncomfortable at the distance which was growing between us.

Things got more than a little weird.

Slowly, over time, Shelley and I noticed that Terry started to flirt with the Dark Side. It wasn't long before she, too, waltzed off to the land of the happily married with Chris. Of course, Shelley and I were privately singing, "Another one bites the dust." We were so burned out on the whole guy scene—and it didn't help matters to see how happy Denise and Terry were.

Shelley was the next to go. When she met David, I knew she was a goner. All I heard was, "David this" and "David that" until I wanted to pull out every strand of her legally blonde hair. Sure, I wanted to be happy for her. But the band was now moving into unfamiliar territory. Three of us were married.

And there I was, approaching my mid-twenties . . . alone.

I was the odd one out.

Complicating my feelings of isolation was the reality that as you get older, you need to make some key life decisions.

Where do I settle down?

Do I keep renting, or do I buy a condo?

Do I buy furniture and decorate, or do I wait?

I had always believed that by the time those issues rolled around, I would have a husband to help sort things out. After all, those choices are hard enough when you have a spouse, but even harder when you're on your own. I was devastated.

I remember sitting on the steps of the condo that I wanted to purchase, heartbroken. From the very depths of my heart and soul, I longed for that special

✳

someone. With unabashed honesty, I cried out to Jesus, "Lord, where are you? Why am I doing this on my own? If you won't provide my heart's desire, then change my heart. Take away the desire for a husband."

I came to the point of confessing that I wasn't completely trusting him. Worse, my lack of trust was making me miserable. I got down on my knees and asked for forgiveness and prayed that he would fill the emptiness. As I sat there, wiping my tears with the cuff of my shirt sleeve, it was as if I heard a whisper in my ear: "God has said, 'Never will I leave you; never will I forsake you'" (Heb. 13:5b).

I'd like to say that within seconds a handsome, godly neighbor walked by, sensed my hurt, comforted me—and that we got married the next day. But God doesn't work like that. He knew I needed *plenty* of time alone.

I needed a season of growth.

I needed a time to go far deeper in my spiritual walk with him than I ever dreamed possible. Looking back, I see how God used my pain to teach me things I might never had learned without a journey through the desert.

One of those treasures was a promise buried in the Old Testament. Like a cup of refreshing water, I drank deeply from the words recorded by the prophet

✳

Isaiah: "'Though the mountains be shaken and the hills be removed, yet my unfailing love for you will not be shaken nor my covenant of peace be removed,' says the Lord, who has compassion on you" (54:10).

Are you wandering through a desert of loneliness? Have your carefully crafted plans failed? Does it feel as if God has forgotten you? Do you wonder if maybe, just maybe, he has misplaced your file? Take heart from someone who knows what you're going through. Better yet, remember the promises of God. He will meet you. Right where you are—in the good times and in the bad.

His love will never change.
Sure as the steady rain.
Jesus will still be there.

As the story unfolded, about one and a half years after I sat on the steps of the condo, Brian and I were married. God's timing was so perfect and I am blessed to have Brian in my life. The truth is, even now, when the storms come, when the rains wash out our plans, when our path isn't clear, I find myself looking over my shoulder to draw strength from the lessons learned in the desert.

We are never alone. We have God's word on that.

✳

Keep *the* Candle Burning

Describe a longing of your heart. Why might a loving heavenly Father make you wait to receive the fulfillment of that desire? What advice does King David give two times in Psalm 27:14?

_____

_____

_____

_____

_____

_____

_____

_____

_____

_____

_____

_____

_____

_____

✳

Faith, Hope, and Love
Terry Jones

There's a tale about a young man named Billy. As the story goes, he and his family lived at the base of the Rocky Mountains in Colorado. One sunny morning, this seventeen-year-old hiked up a trail that was dangerously close to the edge of the mountain. After several hours of rugged climbing he reached the summit, about fourteen thousand feet above sea level.

From the top, he could just about see Kansas with the naked eye. He was basking in the coolness, enjoying the view, when he began to feel the effects of the high altitude. Light-headed, he had trouble breathing. He knew the sun would set before he returned home unless he hurried. Fighting off the dizziness, he began a quick descent.

In his haste, Billy's foot slipped and he tumbled

*

over the edge of the bluff. Fortunately, a tree limb jutting out from the cliff broke his fall. Cut and bruised, he clung to the branch for dear life. Once he stabilized himself, he considered his options. He quickly determined there was no way to climb up the smooth face of the mountainside.

He stole a glance downward. Not good.

The next outcropping had to be at least a hundred feet below. If he lost his grip, he'd fall to his death—of that he was certain. The sun was starting to ease itself into the horizon. If he didn't get help soon, he'd spend the night dangling from the branch—that is, if he had the strength to hold on.

Billy cried out, "HELP! Is anybody there?"

His voice echoed through the canyon. No answer.

He called again. "Somebody . . . anybody . . . HELP!"

A moment later he heard a voice say, "Yes? What is it?"

"I'm down here," Billy yelled, struggling to hold on. "Who's that?"

"It's God, Billy."

Billy wasn't a religious young man, but if God was there to help, he'd take the assistance.

"Listen, God, if you get me out of this, I promise to—"

✳

"Easy on the promises," God said. "Don't worry. I'll get you down. I promise."

"Please, help me. I can't hold on much longer."

"I understand your situation," God said. "But, do you trust me, Billy?"

"Sure," he said, as his fingernails dug into the bark. "I trust you. Now please, just hurry. I'll do anything."

"Good, then I want you to let go of the branch," God said.

Puzzled, Billy figured the altitude was playing games with his mind. "Um, it sounded like you said I should let go."

"Yes, Billy. If you trust me, just let go."

After a long minute, Billy cried out, "HELP! Is there anybody else up there?"

I just love that story because it reminds me how much I am like Billy. I claim to trust in the Lord to provide, but only if he provides in a way that makes sense to me. Let me share a very personal example.

When I was in high school, my father, as the head of a company where he had only recently taken a job, was sent to prison for some business-related practices that occurred before his arrival. My family was devastated. Not only was it unfair for Dad to serve time for something he hadn't done, but now

✳

20

we were without his income. How would we pay our bills? How would we eat and keep the lights on?

My mom took a job, but she didn't make enough to make ends meet. It was such a difficult time, and yet it was a time when we learned to rely on our faith in God; we had a hope that his love would carry us through. Naturally, as a teenager, I remember thinking that if I were God, I would have had a judge release my dad and everything would be okay.

But God had other plans to provide for us. For three and a half long years, as we put our faith, hope, and trust in him, checks would appear in the mailbox from people we didn't know. Others stepped up to provide mechanical services for our cars, odd jobs around the house, and emotional support for us all. Every Christmas, friends from church made sure we received Christmas dinner with all the trimmings and my three sisters and I were given gifts. It was so amazing to watch God work in that situation—once we let go and put our trust in him.

Meanwhile, my dad, a solid Christian man, used his time to bring revival to those around him in prison. Even to this day, Dad has a full-time ministry to prisoners.

No wonder I love the words found in Psalm 121. Listen to this wonderful promise. "I lift my eyes to

*

the hills—where does my help come from? My help comes from the LORD, the Maker of heaven and earth. He will not let your foot slip—he who watches over you will not slumber . . . the LORD will keep you from all harm—he will watch over your life" (v. 1–3, 7).

How long will it take for me to get that message through my thick skull? Why do I so easily forget to trust the promises of my Savior? Yes, no matter what you are going through. No matter how dire the circumstances, or how black the night looks, he invites you to rest in his arms. He longs for you to put your faith, hope, and trust in him, who is able to keep you from all harm.

Are you hanging on to life by a thread?

Unlike Billy, just let go and let God be God.

✳

Keep *the* Candle Burning

Of the twelve disciples, Thomas had difficulty placing his trust in the claims of Jesus. In John 20:27, what did Jesus invite Thomas to do? What's stopping you from doing the same today?

_____

_____

_____

_____

_____

_____

_____

_____

_____

_____

_____

_____

_____

_____

_____

✳

I Have No Doubt
Denise Jones

I was raised in the church and invited Jesus into my life when I was six. I'd like to say everything since then has been rosy, but, as you'll see in a minute, that wouldn't be true. I'd like to tell you I always know exactly what the Lord is up to in my life. The truth? Sometimes God just doesn't make sense to me.

Does that sound irreverent? Unspiritual?

Maybe a touch unfitting for a Christian to say?

Here's the good news. I've learned God is not fragile. He isn't insecure. He doesn't cover his ears and run into the other room for fear we might level with him . . . or bring our deepest heartfelt doubts to him. Quite the opposite. He welcomes our questions with open arms.

Just look at King David.

✳

David began Psalm 13 with this plea: "How long, O Lord? Will you forget me forever? How long will you hide your face from me? How long must I wrestle with my thoughts and every day have sorrow in my heart? How long will my enemy triumph over me?"

How many times in just those two verses did David, pounding his fists against the doors of heaven, ask God, "How long?" I counted four. What was God's response? Did he send a bolt of lightning to put David back in line? Hardly.

As if David hadn't already pushed his welcome, in verse 3 he says, "Look on me and answer, O LORD my God." I'd say that's pretty bold stuff. Then again, I can't blame David for one second. Like David, I've exchanged more than my share of honest words with God.

Not long ago, my husband, Stu, and I had a brush with death. At the time, we had a two-year-old and a brand-new baby. Stu began to experience severe hip trouble. As much as he wanted to blow it off as no big deal, the pain for him became unbearable. We had no choice but to seek medical help. The doctors ran a battery of tests and discovered a tumor in his thighbone.

Our doctor, speaking in gentle, assuring tones, informed us the tumor could be cancerous. Even

✳

though softly spoken, the moment the word *cancer* rolled off of his tongue, a thousand emotions whirled through my pounding heart. I was instantly dizzy with fear.

What? My husband . . . with cancer?

No way. If he had cancer, he might die. I was terrified at the prospect of being left a single mom with two young kids. For the next five days, we were forced to wait on a new batch of tests that would determine if the tumor was malignant. While we waited for the results, the band was in the studio and I was scheduled to do a solo. Talk about timing.

I hit bottom the next morning while riding in the car to record my part. I couldn't stop the flood of tears. How could I sing confidently about a loving, all-powerful God when my heart was so filled with doubt? Where was he in the midst of our situation? Why would God give me a wonderful husband and two children, only to pull the rug out from under us?

I didn't hear an audible voice.

There was no handwriting in the sky.

But God met me there—as real as if he were in the seat beside me. Jesus impressed these words upon my heart: "No matter what the outcome, Denise, I am here with you. Trust me." It was such an unforgettable, supernatural moment. He heard my cries.

✳

He wasn't too busy with world affairs to take time out for me.

Five days passed. I couldn't contain myself when we learned the tumor was benign. Praise God, Stu is doing great. But there was another aspect to the healing process.

You know what? I learned I could go, like David, into the throne room of the King of kings and get an audience. Actually, I got far more than an audience from a benevolent ruler.

I received the embrace of a loving Father.

I came away from that difficult season in my life a changed person. As the song says, "I have no doubt, no matter where you take me, that nothing can separate me from You, Lord." I also came to understand that God never promised us a perfect world, perfect health, or perfect relationships.

At least, not now. That will come when he returns to usher in a new heaven and a new earth. Meanwhile, are you struggling with uncertainty? With doubt? With worry? With unemployment? Are you afraid to get painfully honest with God? Take heart.

He already knows what you're going through.

And he's longing to meet you, no matter where you are.

Even in your car.

✳

Have you ever, like David, been painfully honest with God when difficult circumstances came your way? If not, why not? What steps might you take to enter the throne room of God with greater conviction and honesty?

_____

_____

_____

_____

_____

_____

_____

_____

_____

_____

_____

_____

_____

_____

_____

✳

No More Pain
Heather Payne

Have you ever darted into a grocery store just to buy one gallon of milk? I have and I've often wondered why they put it all the way in the far corner. My guess is they've designed the store to make you walk past a hundred other yummy things to buy.

And have you ever noticed how much shelf space is dedicated to medicine in the pharmacy section? I did the other day and it seems there's a pill, syrup, or cream for everything. Headache. Backache. Tummy ache. Foot ache. Sinus pain. Arthritis pain. Gastrointestinal pain. Sore throat. Sunburn. Skin rash. Diaper rash. Muscle rub. Poison-ivy itch. There's even itch mite cream. Whew!

And I'm just getting started.

We have so many ways to medicate our aches and pain, don't we? Pain is, after all, such a pain.

Let me ask you what might seem like an odd question. Have you ever thanked God while you were in pain? I'm serious. In 1 Thessalonians 5:18 we're told to "Give thanks in all circumstances, for this is God's will for you in Christ Jesus." All circumstances? Even when I'm experiencing a pounding headache? Even when I'm in pain?

Apparently, yes. But why? Wouldn't a pain-free life be far more awesome?

Actually, no.

A life devoid of physical pain would literally kill us.

Think about it. Without pain, how would you know to pull your hand away from a hot oven? How would you know if you sat on a tack, stepped on a nail, or stubbed your toe? Without pain, how would you avoid disfiguring your hand if a car door slammed on your fingers?

Dr. Paul Brand wrote an amazing book a number of years ago with Philip Yancey called *Pain: The Gift Nobody Wants.* Dr. Brand was born in India, where his parents served as medical missionaries. As you might expect from someone living in that part of the world, he saw countless cases of leprosy.

In time, he became a hand surgeon and an expert

✳

in pain. Like his parents, Dr. Brand dedicated much of his life to working among the lepers in India. He was especially fascinated by their inability to feel pain. After much study, he concluded leprosy was not a "rotting flesh" disease as previously thought.

Leprosy was a disease of the nervous system.

Without going into all of the details, he spent fifty years studying the problem. He determined pain was an indicator—a warning light—that informs our bodies something isn't quite right and needs our immediate attention. Lepers, he discovered, first lose the ability to feel pain through damage to their nerves. In turn, they might step on sharp objects, cut their feet, suffer infection, and ultimately lose the use of the limb.

We need pain to live, or we die.

So, yes, I thank God for pain.

Pain also serves an even greater purpose: it can drive us to Jesus, the Great Physician. I love the story in Mark 5:24b–29 about a woman who suffered incredible pain for many years. Read with me how her pain drove her to the Savior.

A large crowd followed and pressed around [Jesus]. And a woman was there who had been subject to bleeding for twelve years. She had suffered a great

✳

deal under the care of many doctors and had spent all she had, yet instead of getting better she grew worse. When she heard about Jesus, she came up behind him in the crowd and touched his cloak, because she thought, "If I just touch his clothes, I will be healed." Immediately her bleeding stopped and she felt in her body that she was freed from her suffering.

Now, look at the reaction of Jesus.

At once Jesus realized that power had gone out from him. He turned around in the crowd and asked, "Who touched my clothes?"

Her heart must have been on the verge of exploding. She was busted. She had been caught stealing a healing. We read she "came and fell at his feet and, trembling with fear, told him the whole truth" (v. 33).

Now, here's one of those 'I-can't-believe-I-opened-my-big-fat-mouth' comments from Peter. He said, "Master, the people are crowding and pressing against you" (Luke 8:45). Peter, for whatever reason, felt compelled to help Jesus get the big picture. I imagine he probably put his arm around Jesus as he explained, "Um, Lord, remember, there's, like, this really big crowd surrounding us?"

Peter missed the point.

Jesus was fully aware who had touched him.

He didn't ask for his benefit, but for the benefit of those around him. Jesus had been touched countless times by the crowd. And yet it had been just this one poor woman—motivated by pain—who had sought his healing power. After her confession, Jesus affirmed her, saying, "Daughter, your faith has healed you. Go in peace and be free from your suffering" (Mark 5:34).

Are you experiencing physical pain today? Take heart. Maybe this is just the perfect opportunity to go deeper with the Savior. What about medication to ease the discomfort? I'm all for it. What about medicine that stimulates the healing process when I'm sick? Ask my husband. I'll be the first one in the prescription line. At the same time, I know I'm trying to learn how to rejoice in all things.

I also yearn for the coming day in which God has promised that pain will no longer be a necessary part of living. The Scripture says, "He will wipe away every tear from their eyes. There will be no more death or mourning or crying or pain" (Rev. 21:4). What's more, as the song says, "It won't be long 'til Jesus comes back." Talk about great news!

Meanwhile, the next time you reach for the bottle of aspirin at the grocery store, try something different.

Try giving thanks, too.

✳

Point of Grace

In John 11:4, what was the purpose of Lazarus' sickness? When was the last time you gave thanks to God while being sick? Why do you think rejoicing in the midst of pain doesn't come naturally for most people?

_____

_____

_____

_____

_____

_____

_____

_____

_____

_____

_____

_____

_____

_____

_____

_____

✳

The Great Divide

Terry Jones

You know, I can't pinpoint the exact date. I can't tell you what the weather was like. I'm not sure I'd even remember what I was wearing at the time. But I'll never forget the face of the woman who appeared at our dressing room door and the amazing story she was dying to tell us. Here's what happened.

Right around the time this song hit the radio, we were scheduled to play at a fairgrounds event in Washington State. After the usual sound check, Heather and I were directed to a tired-looking utility trailer around back, one with the words "Dressing Room" scribbled on a piece of paper and taped to the door. We were getting ready when someone knocked.

Curious, we opened the door and discovered a

*

shy woman standing outside. She asked if she could have just a minute of our time. Frankly, there are times when we are rushed before a concert and don't have the option of visiting with a guest. This, however, was one of those moments when Heather and I sensed the need to be available to her. Unsure what to expect, we welcomed her in.

With a nervous hand she tucked a loose strand of hair behind her ear. She told us how she, for a long time, had struggled with depression. She'd reached the end of her rope. She was forty years old, with two precious children ages eight and nine, and she was convinced her life wasn't worth living.

Fighting back tears, she shared how she had planned to commit suicide earlier *that very week*. Living in the Seattle area, with a number of steep cliffs to choose from, she figured she'd just pick one and run her car over the edge.

What happened next was clearly the hand of God.

This woman, alone and desperate, decided to listen to the radio as she drove in search of a place to crash. As God would have it, "The Great Divide" filled the speakers. As she gripped the steering wheel, her cheeks were stained with streams of sadness. Still, she was struck by the lyric, "He found me

✳

hopeless, alone, and sent a Savior." In that moment, God used those words to spark a tiny flame of hope in her innermost being. She pulled the car over and started to sob as the words washed over her shattered heart.

God loved her so much he took the initiative to love her.

He made a way possible for her to know him.

For her to have peace.

For her to experience a changed heart.

As you can imagine, my pulse was racing as she told us this story. I, too, began to cry tears of joy. Why? Of course I was thrilled for her to come to Christ and to enter into his perfect peace. But there was something more.

I know I'm not the best singer in the world. I'll never have the vocal range of Mariah Carey or Celine Dion. But what I have, I've asked the Lord to use for his glory. Sitting there in front of us that afternoon was living proof of God's grace. The Savior was pleased to use our efforts—as incomplete as they are—to bring this lost sheep into the fold.

I was so blown away.

Looking back on that afternoon, I'm reminded of Isaiah 53:5. The prophet, pointing to the Messiah, said, "But he was pierced for our transgressions, he

✳

was crushed for our iniquities; the punishment that brought us peace was upon him, and by his wounds we are healed."

You see, without Christ, we experience separation from the Creator. It wasn't always that way. In fact, at the beginning of time, God placed us in a perfect world. He longed to walk in the cool of the evening with us. But when Adam and Eve sinned, an insurmountable canyon—the great divide—formed between God and mankind, preventing the intimacy we were designed to have.

Sin separated us from fellowship with God.

The narrative in Genesis 3:23–24 says, "So the LORD banished him from the Garden of Eden to work the ground from which he had been taken. After he drove the man out, he placed on the east side of the Garden of Eden cherubim and a flaming sword flashing back and forth to guard the way to the tree of life."

Thank God the story doesn't end there.

Thanks to Jesus, you and I no longer have to stand in the shadows of a flame-wielding angel, banished from paradise. As the song says, "Sin would still separate us, were it not for the bridge His grace has made us."

Grace.

*

Unmerited favor.

The ultimate blessing.

We don't deserve it. But God, in his amazing love, freely offers us a way back to him. As Isaiah prophesied, Jesus became the bridge across the great divide. I, for one, am eternally thankful the woman who came to see us heard the song, embraced the Good News . . . and lived to tell us about it.

✳

Point of Grace

Why does sin keep us from entering into fellowship with God? What provision did God make for you and me to enter into heaven? What's the most amazing aspect of God's grace?

_____

_____

_____

_____

_____

_____

_____

_____

_____

_____

_____

_____

_____

_____

_____

*

Dying to Reach You
Shelley Breen

My husband and I live in a beautiful suburb of Nashville, Tennessee. Everywhere you look, the large, level yards are accented by lush landscaping. Every hedge is clipped. The flowers grow in neat, weed-free rows. The wide streets are pothole free and shaded by tall, mature trees. The children ride their tricycles in freshly ironed Baby Gap outfits.

And everybody waves, just like in Mayberry.

Okay, so I'm exaggerating a little. Still, compared to the big city, you might say life in Brentwood is like floating on a soft cloud in an endless blue sky. Guess what? Living in this modern Mayberry is enough to drive me insane. Why?

In Brentwood, everything and *everyone* is mani- cured. Day or night, the women all sport a smile and the latest fashion from Talbots. Their nails look professionally polished. Their makeup is flawless. And forget about bad-hair days. They don't exist in Brentwood.

For the life of me I couldn't tell you how the other mothers cope with their kids. They're amazing. Even in the rain, these Super Moms manage to juggle three perfectly groomed children, wearing coordinated outfits, as they zip around in their late-model Suburban to soccer practice or maybe a quick lunch with friends at the Puffy Muffin.

Talk about feeling the pressure.

Me? We're talking sweats. I'm probably the only one in Brentwood who can't find time to iron the baby's socks. Sure, I'll get my nails done—and then promptly snap off a tip as I drag the stroller to the back of the oversized SUV later that same day.

How about you? Do you find yourself caught up in the endless battle to look the part? To be the perfect mom? To have a healthy dinner made—on time—when your husband comes home? Or, maybe to dress the family like a page out of *Martha Stewart Living*?

Do you find yourself running on empty, unable to get a grip on life? Are you afraid that someone might just walk into your house, unannounced, clipboard

✳

in hand, to take notes of the mess, the piles of unfolded clothes, and the chaos in the kitchen sink?

I know I do . . . daily.

Here's the trap you and I can fall into if we're not careful. As we scramble to keep the family in picture-perfect shape for that unexpected Kodak Moment, it's easy to become obsessed with always looking the part. We become conditioned to worry about finding the proper window dressing to cover what's really going on inside.

The danger occurs if we allow this obsession to carry over into our relationship with Jesus. How? It's a subtle thing. It happens slowly over time. Before we know it, we want to make sure we've got it all together. We dare not let Jesus drop by our heart's door, unannounced, and see us for who we really are.

I don't know about you, but it's easy for me to feel as if he expects me to straighten up the mess in my soul before I come into his presence. If I'm not careful, I'll believe the lie that I must make sure there's no soap scum in the sink of my spirit before I welcome him home.

You know, there's a simple, yet powerful line in this song that helps me regain my perspective: "So come as you are."

✳

Wow! That's so cool. I don't have to pretend that I've got it all together—which I don't. I don't have to rearrange the furniture, dust the corners, or vacuum the carpet before he comes inside. I don't need to be embarrassed at what he might find *if only he knew.*

When I remember that Jesus died for me, that he offered himself as a perfect sacrifice on my behalf, and that he loves me unconditionally, even in my imperfect, sinful state, then I'm released from the false pressure to clean up my act, or to look the part.

Does that sound too good to be true? Is it really possible that Jesus loves me so much that I don't have to hesitate to enjoy his fellowship? In John 6:37b, Jesus says, "whoever comes to me I will never drive away."

Whoever includes you and me. *Never* means under no circumstance—not when our soul's dark with anger. Not when we have questions, even doubts, about what God is doing in our lives. Nor will he push us away when we're bitter, filled with envy, struggling with lust, or wrestling with depression.

Never means never.

Jesus will never, ever wipe a gloved finger along the edges of my heart and announce, "There's dirt here, Shelley. So, you can just forget about my love."

That's the freedom he's dying for you and me to

✳

know. That's the freedom that can only come through what Jesus did for us.

I love what one woman said: "Ain't no makeup gonna cover the blemish on your soul, honey. So give it up."

Have you been afraid to let Jesus get close? To know your innermost struggles? To love you unconditionally? To embrace you with the everlasting arms of divine love?

Then, come as you are.

Even in Brentwood.

✳

Point of Grace

Have you been tempted to get your act together before you admit Jesus into the most inner part of your heart? Why? Is there something you wish you could sweep under the rug before Jesus gets close? What awesome promise does 1 John 1:9 offer?

_____

_____

_____

_____

_____

_____

_____

_____

_____

_____

_____

_____

_____

_____

_____

_____

✳

46

Gather at the River
Heather Payne

I became a Christian when I was nine years old. That morning, my mom had pulled my brown hair back into two neat little ponytails that bobbed as I walked to the front of the room during children's church. Nervous yet excited, I stood with the others who had made the same decision. Those first, innocent steps of faith set me on an amazing pilgrimage. This journey of discovery has been a quest to know more about the awesome God who loved and died for me.

Now, more than twenty years later, I've read the stories in my Bible many times. I've studied under some really great teachers and preachers. I'm even married to a minister. So, what else is there to know? Honestly, it's easy for me to become complacent. But just when I think I've dug deep enough,

*

Jesus boggles my mind with a precious gem I've missed.

Take the story of the paralytic in Matthew 9.

In a nutshell, here's what happened. We're told a couple of guys brought their buddy, a paralyzed man, to Jesus to be healed. It's worth mentioning that at this point in Jesus' ministry, the word was out on the streets: Jesus could heal *anybody* of *anything*. Nothing was too difficult for him to cure. Thanks to Jesus, demons had been cast out.

Blind men could see.

A man with leprosy had been healed.

We're not talking about small potatoes here.

Listen to the amazing events which led up to Jesus' encounter with the paralytic. Matthew 4:23–24 says, "Jesus went throughout Galilee, teaching in their synagogues, preaching the good news of the kingdom, and healing every disease and sickness among the people. News about him spread all over Syria, and people brought to him all who were ill with various diseases, those suffering from severe pain, the demon-possessed, the epileptics and the paralytics, and he healed them."

Several chapters later, we're introduced to the paralytic. Picture that paralyzed man, lying on a mat at the feet of Jesus. His big day had arrived. His heart was probably on the verge of exploding in expectation. Would Jesus heal him, too? Somehow his friends had managed to push their way through the anxious crowds, through the mass of humanity who, like him, hoped just to touch the hem of Jesus' garment.

We're not told, but maybe he was born paralyzed. Maybe he had an accident that left him in that condition. Whatever his story, he now lay in the shadow of the one he had heard about. The one who had healed so many times before. The one who would, hopefully, give him the mobility he longed for every waking moment.

All eyes were on Jesus. What would this legendary miracle worker do? Would he utter a few healing words? Would he raise his eyes to heaven, say a prayer, and then clap his hands, pronouncing, "Be healed"?

Look closely at what Jesus did first. In Matthew 9:2b, he said, "Take heart, son; your sins are forgiven."

Huh? If I were the guy, I'd be thinking, "Well, that's nice to know, but, um, I was kind of hoping to walk."

We usually look at healing as primarily a function of becoming physically whole. It's about wellness. About tossing the crutches in the trash—preferably in front of the cameras for all to see and gasp in

✳

amazement. But guess what? We've missed something deeper. Something far more significant than flesh and bones functioning as they were intended.

What's going on here?

Jesus knew what this man really needed: *he needed to be forgiven.* More than anything—more than the ability to walk—he needed the ability to leap in the knowledge he could stand before the Lord of hosts as a forgiven man. Yes, Jesus ultimately healed him of the paralysis (v. 6). But let's not forget the primary treasure buried in this account: Jesus wants to do so much more for you and me.

How about you? Have there been times in your life where you've looked to Jesus for physical healing but overlooked what he might want to do on a deeper level in the midst of your suffering? Why is it that we race to him to cure our ills, but fail to ask him to heal our broken relationships? Our troubled marriages? Our pettiness? Our need to experience his forgiveness afresh?

I remember when Shelley, Denise, Terry, and I were having one of those rare fights in the studio. With the pressure of finishing the album on time, we had let petty things fester—right as we were about to sing this song! Boy, did we need to drink deeply at the "fountain from the Mercy Giver."

✳

Isn't it amazing how Jesus knows exactly what we need, when we need it? So, today, come to the river. Cast your cares on him for he cares for you. Whether you're nine years old and just beginning the walk of faith, or ninety-nine with your eyes set on glory, as the song says, "there's redemption at the riverside."

And don't be too surprised if he heals more than you've asked for!

✳

Point of Grace

*W*hen we pray to be made well, we usually pray for physical healing. What does God want to heal in his people in Acts 28:27? List several non-physical areas where you would like to experience the healing touch of Christ.

_____

_____

_____

_____

_____

_____

_____

_____

_____

_____

_____

_____

_____

_____

✳

God *Is* With Us
Terry Jones

Do you know what I want so badly? I want my three kids never to grow up. Ever. If I could, I'd freeze life right where they are at this delightful young stage. I want to pamper them silly. I want them always to know love. Maybe you've had some of those same feelings, too.

For me, I identify with the mother hen who keeps her young safe and snug under her wings. I yearn to keep my babies away from the craziness, the uncertainty, the hurt, and the dangers that await them at every corner.

And yet I know, hour by hour, they inch forward to a time when they will leave the safety of my arms. I may not be able to hold back the hands of time. But I can do for them what my parents did for me—I can

✳

introduce my children to faith in Jesus at a very young age.

What better gift is there?

Looking back, I recall my parents became Christians when I was pretty young—maybe five or six years old. Dad had this idea we should go to a family camp in California called Mount Herman. The gorgeous campground was set in the shadows of these enormous, majestic redwood trees. The soft, delightful scent of pinecones filled the air.

The moment we arrived, my three sisters and I jumped out of the family car and right into tons of fun classes, activities, crafts, and sports. While we were off doing our thing, my parents were listening to great speakers and enjoying adult-type stuff. Then at night, we'd all come back together and have family time around the campfire.

I'll never forget the drive home from camp. We had learned so much about God that week, more than at any time in my short six years. I should mention that prior to this camp experience, my family and I had been to church—not a lot, mind you. But we'd visit from time to time. Even so, we didn't really have any idea who God was or who Jesus was or what he did for us.

As we drove down the road, my sisters and I sang

✳

songs that spoke of having "Jesus in our hearts"—
you know, the songs we had learned at camp. At one
point, Dad asked us if we knew what those words
meant. We looked at each other and admitted, no,
not really.

I guess Dad sensed that was a teachable moment.
Rather than press on to get home, he eased the car
over to the side of the road. We parked at the base
of these amazing redwoods. Under the covering of
those tall pine trees, Dad started to ask us a bunch
of questions about what we had learned that week.
Then, in very simple terms, he explained the gospel
message to us.

Dad made John 3:16 come alive. "For God so
loved the world that he gave his one and only Son,
that whoever believes in him shall not perish but
have eternal life." Dad explained how Jesus had to die
on a cross, in our place, because of this love for us.

For me. Wow!

Dad made it clear that this wasn't about joining a
church. It was about an ongoing *relationship* with
Jesus, who wanted to be part of our daily lives.

Not just on Sundays.

Not just in our heads.

Not just at camp.

Or just when things were going smoothly.

✳

Jesus longed to live in our hearts. For all time.

I'd like to say a burst of fireworks blasted off inside my little six-year-old head. Nope. But what Dad said made a whole lot of sense. For the first time, my sisters and I came to understand, as the song says, "God is with us." God was with me. Yes, Jesus loved me. He wanted to be my Savior and my friend.

When Dad asked if we wanted to accept Jesus into our lives, we all did! The four of us girls invited Christ into our hearts—right there in the car.

That tender moment represented my first baby steps in this journey of faith. A journey I now share with my own three little cherubs. Yes, I want to savor these days with my kids. But more than that, I want them to know about this God who, "though the night is long, and the river's strong," will be with them, too.

And, as the song says, whenever the "river deepens, night grows darker, and the struggle seems to be getting harder," I trust my kids will have learned that "He will cover you with his feathers, and under his wings you will find refuge; his faithfulness will be your shield and rampart" (Ps. 91:4).

Yes, God is with me. With them. With us.

✳

Frankly, I'm bracing myself because I know the day is coming—sooner than I care to imagine—when my kids will leave our cozy nest, spread their wings, and take flight on their own. Before they do, I plan to use the little teachable moments along the highway of life to point them to Jesus.

Just as my dad did for me.

*

Point of Grace

Does going to church automatically make you a Christian? What, then, is necessary to experience salvation? Have you taken that step? If not, what's stopping you?

_____

_____

_____

_____

_____

_____

_____

_____

_____

_____

_____

_____

_____

_____

_____

*

Love Like No Other
Shelley Breen

I have a confession to make.

Shortly after my daughter was born, I honestly thought I had made a huge mistake. There. I said it. Don't get me wrong, Caroline is beautiful and I love her more than life itself. But in those first panicked moments, I had no idea in the world how I'd be able to manage two babies at once—little Caroline *and* my wonderful husband, David, who, at times, seems to need extra pampering.

I even told David I was sure I'd have to quit the band. How could I fly to our concerts with an infant? He acted like I was nuts and told me simply to bring the baby along. Right.

Take a newborn on the road?

With our schedule?

I'd like to see *him* juggle a diaper bag, stroller,

bottles, and a crying child through security check-points where they strip-search you at least twice before you get on the plane.

Thankfully, those days of postpartum blues are behind me. I can't imagine life without her. As a matter of fact, I'd do anything to protect her. Sometimes when I watch the news and see all of the crazy stuff going on in our world, I hold her in my arms just a little bit tighter. In my heart of hearts, I long to shelter her from all harm. That's why, for the life of me, I cannot fathom the accounts of mothers who abuse their children. I'm sure you've seen the same stories.

The woman who hit her child in a superstore parking lot.

The mom who drowned her kids in a bathtub.

The woman who locked her children in a basement for days.

The sick mother who took graphic pictures of her kids to sell on the Internet.

But just when I begin to wonder what this world is coming to, I stumble onto a bittersweet story of a mother's unconditional love that thaws the chill in my spirit.

According to the news account, Ronald and Tayne Ferris owned a car dealership in New Hampshire. It

✳

was a Sunday afternoon in March and the couple, along with their five sons, were flying home from Florida in a small plane. What was supposed to be a routine flight turned into a deadly nightmare. As they approached the New England region, covered in a thick blanket of fresh snow, the outside air temperatures plummeted.

Ice began to form on the wings.

Rather than take a chance, the pilot radioed air-traffic control to schedule an emergency landing in Massachusetts. His last radio contact was at 6:50 P.M. as the frosty night approached. When they didn't reach the airport, rescue teams were dispatched at daybreak the next morning to search the mountainous area.

Eighteen hours after the distress call, the family's plane, which had plowed into the side of Mount Wilcox, was discovered. Rescuers were lowered to the site by a helicopter—just in case. But what were the chances anybody could survive a crash at that altitude and in that arctic-like weather? Remarkably, three of the couple's children survived the crash.

Sitting in the warmth of my home as I read this account, I wondered how a two-, five-, and ten-year-old made it through the night without gloves, hats,

✳

or other means of staying warm. The answer still takes my breath away.

Tayne Ferris pulled herself over her vulnerable children to shelter them against the storm. The rescue workers found two of the boys cradled beneath her body and they figured the third child had been equally protected, but left the fuselage at the sound of the helicopter.

She died so they would live.

What a display of unconditional love.

In many ways, that's the picture we see of our Savior in Luke 13:34. Jesus said, "O Jerusalem, Jerusalem, you who kill the prophets and stone those sent to you, *how often I have longed to gather your children together, as a hen gathers her chicks under her wings,* but you were not willing" [emphasis added]. Let that sink in.

Jesus loves you and me that much. He longs to shelter us under the protection of his outstretched arms. Yes, his love for us drove him to a cross.

Not because we've done something to deserve his affection.

Not because we have anything to offer him in exchange.

The only explanation I can point to is the uncon-

✳

ditional love of our heavenly Father. His life for mine. With no strings attached. Thanks to Jesus, we can have life eternal with him. As the song says, "It's beyond all reason, it's a love I'll never understand."

That, my friend, is a love like no other.

✳

Point of Grace

What motivated Jesus to lay down his life for us on the cross? Why does Jesus love you unconditionally? How might you express your thanks to him for this gift of love?

_____

_____

_____

_____

_____

_____

_____

_____

_____

_____

_____

_____

_____

_____

_____

_____

*

Keep the Candle Burning

Denise Jones

I am not a very organized person. Sure, I'd like to have a picture-perfect home environment. The kind of place where the toys are on the shelves after playtime. Clothes are folded in the drawers. Shoes are lined up by the door. Dishes are put away after meals. But with me? Fat chance. I struggle more than other people just to keep things picked up.

I remember I was barely maintaining my head above water when the storm hit. Literally. In January of 2003, Nashville got socked by one of the worst snowstorms in its history: seven inches of snow. Okay, if you live in the Northeast, you're probably laughing right about now. What's the big deal with a few inches?

Let's just say that here, school is cancelled on the mere *prediction* of any precipitation. That makes

✳

seven inches of snow a downright blizzard. It shuts down the town. We're talking a storm of abominable snowman proportions.

So there I was, cooped up and snowed in with two rowdy boys, two and five years old, all morning long. For hours, they zipped around my ankles kicking up a cloud of dust in their wake. The house was in a state of complete bedlam. Toys covered every inch of the floor. Dishes piled up.

And the phone was ringing.

Under normal levels of chaos, I'd just let the answering machine grab the message. That particular day, however, I remember scurrying around to find the handset—buried somewhere in the mess— just in case it was the doctor.

You see, my mother-in-law was staying with us for several weeks recovering from hip replacement surgery. Unable to use stairs, and without a bedroom on the first floor, my husband, Stu, and I set up a hospital bed in our living room for her use. Whenever the phone rang, I knew it might be one of three important people calling to schedule visits: the therapist, the doctor, or the nurse.

Complicating matters was the fact I was not used to helping change my mother-in-law's clothes. It's not like she's that old. She doesn't have dementia

✳

and was somehow unaware of what I was doing. It was awkward, to say the least. On top of that, I didn't know which medication to give her because my husband forgot to provide me with that little detail.

With my house in a wreck, the kids playing wild Indians, a Lego lodged in my foot, and the phone ringing, I just wanted to stand up and scream. I was so ready to just totally lose it. I'm telling you, it was one of those meltdown moments. I felt as if I were living in the core of a nuclear reactor.

Of course, who do I take it out on? My poor husband. Like a deer caught in the headlights, he got the brunt of it. I mean I really unloaded both barrels. I finally had to excuse myself and go in the other room. I remember pouring out my heart to the Lord. I said, "Jesus, I simply cannot deal with this—not for another second."

You know what? Jesus met me there.

In my weakness.

At the end of my rope.

When the clouds had darkened my view.

Yes, in my frailty, he wrapped his mighty arms around me. I was alone, frustrated, and ready to combust spontaneously, and yet it was as if Jesus had spoken those words of old just for my benefit: "Peace, be still."

✳

Peace, be still.

I took a deep breath as he quieted the storm in my soul. Although I didn't hear an audible voice, I heard him say, "Denise, the people in your life are more important than the things you have got to get done."

Immediately, I felt the weight fly off of my shoulders. At that very moment, I knew two things.

He was there with me in the midst of the storm.

He would be there as I loved and served my family.

Jesus would help me keep from trampling on their tender spirits in the process. The stuff would get done sooner or later. No way would I allow my short fuse to blow up in their precious faces.

Yes, Jesus was there, as real as the snow blanketing the trees outside of my window.

Why am I so surprised? I'm no different than the disciples crowding around a sleeping Jesus in the bottom of the boat where he laid his tired head. Mark 4:38 says, "Jesus was in the stern, sleeping on a cushion. The disciples woke him and said to him, 'Teacher, don't you care if we drown?'"

Think about their question. Kind of silly, huh? Sure, all around them, they watched as the waves of the storm threatened to capsize their little world. And yet, the one who formed the oceans in the palm

✳

of his hand was within reach. They just needed to ask.

Verse 39 tells us, "He got up, rebuked the wind and said to the waves, 'Quiet! Be still!' Then the wind died down and it was completely calm." Here's the amazing part of the story. In verse 41, we read, "They were terrified and asked each other, 'Who is this? Even the wind and the waves obey him!'"

Did you catch it? They were more terrified by Jesus' display of power than by the storm which they, just a split second earlier, were convinced would kill them.

How about you? Are you feeling overwhelmed today? Are the waves of your circumstances crashing all around you? Do you think there's no hope? Have you lost sight of his endless power? As the song says, "the Lord is gonna see you through."

Just don't wait for a snowstorm before you ask.

✳

W hat stresses you out the most in life? Is it a particular person? A situation? Disorder? Financial pressure? What reoccurring promise does God make in Deuteronomy 31:6, Joshua 1:5, Psalm 94:14, Isaiah 42:16, and Hebrews 13:5?

_____

_____

_____

_____

_____

_____

_____

_____

_____

_____

_____

_____

_____

_____

✳

You Are the Answer

Terry Jones

As I see it, the biggest struggle as a parent is finding balance. How much time do I invest in my children, my husband, my church, my circle of friends, and my "to do" list? Once I start to divvy it up, I find there simply isn't enough time for everything in a day. Family life is that demanding.

Not to mention the need to leave time for myself.

I think we mothers often give until we have nothing left. Giving isn't a choice. It comes with the territory. I have to feed my children, bathe them, clothe them, and get them to where they need to be.

Of course, it seems the minute I pick things up around the house, they're all back out again. The second I finish lunch it's time to start on dinner. The cycle of activity can be so overwhelming. What troubles me is how my time pressures tend to rob me

✳

of the sweetness of life. I find it a challenge to take time to stop and look at my children in the eyes and listen to them—especially when they pull on my legs five times in two minutes.

Complicating my already frenetic pace of life is a major musical career. For you, maybe it's a full-time job outside of the home. Or volunteer work at a shelter for the homeless. As I'm sure you have experienced, sorting out these competing priorities becomes so complex.

Oh, did I forget to mention the needs of a husband who wants to snuggle, get close, and connect with me? He and I both need that alone time, too. I've come to understand that if our family is going to stay strong, my marriage must remain healthy. And that takes an additional commitment of time.

It's enough to make me want to throw my hands up and cry out to God, *So what's the answer? How do I juggle all of this? What's the point, anyway? Why bother? Is it really worth the effort?*

The prophet Isaiah says, "How gracious he will be when you cry for help! As soon as he hears, he will answer you" (30:19b). Reading that, I want to kick myself for not calling out to God sooner. I remember a time early in our marriage when things were nuts. I cried out to the Lord and God met me in the

✳

eye of the storm. He whispered a suggestion into what was left of my mind: *Get alone with your helpmate.* Really?

So I did.

I'll let you in on our little secret. Ever since that day, this idea of getting alone has really kept Chris and me sane. From time to time we get away for a few days. No kids. No friends. No business. No agenda.

Just the two of us.

Sometimes we'll do an overnight in a city close to home. Not long ago, he and I went to Florida. We had three full days—*alone.* My baby was six months old and this was the first time we were apart for any length of time. Yes, it was so hard to do. But Chris and I needed to do that for *us.*

We sat at the pool with the sun gently warming our tired bodies. I looked in his eyes and thought, *Yeah, now I remember why I married you.* Chris, after all, is so steady. He takes life as it comes while I get stressed and easily overwhelmed. I was reminded how blessed I am to have him in my life.

These treasured, lifesaving getaways have been an oasis of refreshment throughout our marriage. Why? Because they provide a space to listen to each other. To pray, to dream, to laugh, and to actually *sleep* without interruption.

✳

Back home, when things are hard, and crazy, and chaotic, and I'm spending every waking hour juggling the activities of family life, it's easy to become emotionally detached and distant from my husband. Now, whenever my mind fills up with petty stuff, I can go back to that quiet place where Chris and I connected. I use the memory to re-ignite the fire between us.

Of course, if you're single, there's no reason you can't pamper yourself with a personal retreat, too. Whether a trip to the day spa for a massage, or sailing on a cruise, you need a break from the action to rest, restore, and reflect on the one who loves you.

And you know another benefit?

When Chris and I make our marriage a priority, we always experience the fellowship of the Father, too. God breathes refreshment into our spirits. The Lord uses those trips to rejuvenate us. In Psalm 23 David said, "He makes me lie down in green pastures, he leads me beside quiet waters, he restores my soul" (v. 2–3a).

Don't you love the sound of that?

God restores my soul.

His grace covers my imperfect efforts to meet the family's needs. He quiets my fears about the future. And he faithfully irons out my wrinkled perspective.

✳

As the song says, "You are the answer, and the meaning of life."

You know what? I don't have to have all of the answers for the questions swirling around in my mind. I know the one who does. King David writes, "In the day of my trouble I will call to you, for you will answer me" (Ps. 86:7).

Best of all, when I call upon the Lord and seek his face, he never tells me to take a number, stand in line, wait my turn, hold my thought . . . or asks me if I mind being put on hold while he takes another call.

So, what are you waiting for? Make the "call."

And, while you're at it, start planning that retreat!

✳

Point of Grace

Whether married or single, when was the last time you pampered yourself with a trip somewhere fun? Do you ever feel guilty when you relax? Why? How might Psalm 127:2 put rest in perspective?

_____

_____

_____

_____

_____

_____

_____

_____

_____

_____

_____

_____

_____

_____

_____

*

Circle of Friends
Heather Payne

Back when I lived in Nashville, I met and developed a friendship with another girl. She became such a great friend to me. For one thing, we had a lot in common. You name it, we enjoyed talking about it. And she, like me, loved the Lord. She was a person whom I respected highly.

I loved the way she'd write me all of these notes to encourage me. She would quote Scripture and she seemed to have a profound insight into the Word. I especially valued the fact that she seemed genuinely interested in me *for who I was,* not because I happened to be in this band, Point of Grace. In fact, I distinctly remember a comment she made the day we first met. She had said she hoped I wasn't offended, but that she didn't even know who Point of Grace was.

✳

One day, probably a year into our friendship, I was going through an old box of junk . . . cards, letters, fan mail, recipes, that kind of stuff. As I dug through the stack, an envelope caught the corner of my eye. The handwriting looked really familiar. Curious, I pulled it out of the pile.

When I opened it up, I thought, *Oh, look. This is a letter from my good friend. I wonder what it's doing tucked away with the fan mail?* I studied the postmark and noticed it was dated years and years ago—long before I met her. This I had to see. I pulled up a chair and reread her letter.

Now, I should mention that very seldom do we get letters through our fan mail that move you the way this one moved me. As I sat there reading it, I was touched by how beautifully it had been written. It was an incredible expression of encouragement. No wonder I had kept it.

That's when the ugly truth struck me.

Throughout our friendship, my friend had deceived me.

Way back when we met, she claimed she didn't know who we were. But in truth, she did. She even took the time all those years ago to share with us how our music had impacted her life. Sitting there alone in that room holding her note, I was devas-

✳

tated. This person whom I had trusted with so much had built a friendship on deception.

After the initial shock, I put myself in her place. I tried to imagine why she didn't tell me the truth up front. Maybe she was intimidated by being close to someone whom she had previously watched from afar. Maybe she thought I'd treat her like a fan rather than a friend. Or maybe she just didn't know a comfortable way to explain her interest in us in the past. Whatever her reasons, she had lied to me and it hurt. Deeply.

I felt as if I had been violated. Her lack of honesty and integrity caused me to second-guess our entire friendship. What else might have been a fabrication? How could I trust her to be truthful in the future?

Several things can happen when you've been deceived in that way. Some people refuse to trust another person ever again. That's an extreme reaction but, in a way, I can understand it. Others shy away from anyone who attempts to get close. They suspect ulterior motives. There are also those who take their hurt and turn around and carry that baggage into other relationships.

Are these the only options?

Thank God there's another route to take: the pathway to restoration and healing. As a kid, I was

✳

taught if you fall off your bike, the best thing to do is hop back on and try again. That's kind of what Jesus was driving at when he said, "If your brother sins against you, go and show him his fault, just between the two of you. If he listens to you, you have won your brother over" (Matt. 18:15).

As best I could, I went to her and lovingly confronted her with the letter. I wanted her to drop the charade and to know, as the song says, "no matter what you feel inside, there's no reason to pretend, that's the way it is in this circle of friends."

Without hesitation, she acknowledged writing it. She knew she was in the wrong and asked for my forgiveness. We mended our fences and, while we're not as close as before, we continue to work at our friendship to this day.

Have you been burned by past relationships? Do you find it difficult to reach out to others for fear of being exploited, misunderstood, or deceived?

Whatever you do, don't give up trying to be a friend.

Don't remain off in a corner, isolated.

Forget about going through life alone.

As imperfect as friendships can be, you and I need them. In Galatians 6:2, Paul says, "Carry each other's burdens, and in this way you will fulfill the law of

✳

Christ." You see, when we walk within a circle of friends, we are in a safe place of mutual shelter.

You might be thinking, "Heather, come on, you don't know how badly I've been betrayed. How can you expect me to try trusting a friend again?" You're right. I don't know your situation. But guess what? Jesus does. And yet he still calls us into fellowship, one with another.

Come to think of it, if anybody had a legitimate reason to wash his hands of his friends, it would be Jesus. Why? He was betrayed by much more than an old piece of fan mail.

He was betrayed with a kiss.

✳

Have you ever been betrayed by a friend? How did the betrayal make you feel? Have you forgiven the person? Read Matthew 18:23—35. What does Jesus expect his followers to do regarding forgiveness?

_____

_____

_____

_____

_____

_____

_____

_____

_____

_____

_____

_____

_____

✳

That's the Way It's Meant to Be

Denise Jones

I t was the beginning of the school year. My two
boys were starting back to preschool, and for
unknown reasons, both of them were going
through this huge separation anxiety thing at the
same time. Every morning it was a battle to take
them in to their class. Their bodies stiffened. Their
faces reddened. And they screamed each agonizing
step of the way.

This behavior went on for an entire week.

Now, I'm sure my boys didn't have a private meeting in the back of their bedroom closet in which
they secretly devised a plan to shatter my emotions.
It just worked out that way.

On Friday, you see, the boys clung to my legs for
dear life. Don't ask me how we managed to get
through the front doors. But we did. Inside, their

✳

wailing and hollering reverberated down the hall-way until everyone in the school must have thought I was an awful mother.

I saw the faces of other moms, with their plastic, dazed grins. They hustled their children away from us for fear they might catch whatever was plaguing my boys. The poor teachers rushed to my rescue and then tried, unsuccessfully, to peel them off of me. The staff just about had to resort to using a crowbar to liberate me from the viselike grip of my boys.

Then, a team of teachers held them at bay long enough for me to make my escape around the corner and out of the building. Even outside, their muffled wailing followed me to the car. I collapsed in the front seat.

I had finally had it.

As I drove away, I started to bawl my head off. I actually had to pull off to the side of the road and just let the tears flow. I felt like such a horrible mother. Nobody else would leave their kids like this. What was I doing wrong? Don't they know I love them?

Worse, I felt guilty that maybe, just maybe, I was damaging them for life through the whole ordeal. Talk about hitting rock bottom. Like the song says,

✳

"Everybody has a day when it seems that everything is going nowhere." Or, in my case, going downhill—and fast.

I can tell you that two things pulled me through those dire straits. First, the presence of God. As I sat in my car parked by the side of the road, and as I cried out to the Lord, he heard my cry. I could feel his love wash over me. He assured me I wasn't an awful mom. He was there with me in the midst of my little storm. And he would be with my kids, too. As the Word says, "Cast all your anxiety on him for he cares for you" (1 Pet. 5:7).

You know what? Jesus wouldn't invite you and me to cast our cares on him if he didn't plan to do something with them. In my case, he lifted the burden of guilt from my shoulders and allowed me to bask in his strength to carry on.

I don't remember whom I called that day when my boys almost drove me insane. I do know I called a friend and poured out my heart for probably half an hour. You know what? I wasn't judged. I wasn't lectured. I wasn't patronized. My friend gave me an understanding ear, a supportive heart, a word of encouragement, and a commitment to pray.

Talk about a blessing!

✳

Looking back on that unbearable week with my boys, I can't imagine a life without close friends. It's so true what Ecclesiastes 4:10 says: "If one falls down, his friend can help him up. But pity the man who falls and has no one to help him up!"

Through all of this I gained a fresh appreciation of the value of maintaining friends. Good, solid Christian friends. Not just acquaintances—you know the type, who wave and smile and say, "Call me sometime for lunch," but they never follow through. I'm talking the kind of friend who is "closer than a brother" (Prov. 18:24).

I am so blessed to have that kind of friendship with Shelley, Terry, and Heather. My life is enriched by them. Although we have different gifts, strengths, and weaknesses, our friendship remains strong. As the song says, "we're in it together 'cause that's the way He meant it to be."

How about you?

Can you name one or more friends with whom you can share your burdens? I'm talking about friends who you can contact day or night and know they'll welcome your call? I'm big on this because you and I were designed for fellowship. The apostle John says, "if we walk in the light, as he is in the light, we have fellowship with one an-

✳

other" (1 John 1:7a). Yes, that's the way it's meant to be.

What? You don't think you need anybody else?

Remember this.

Even the Lone Ranger had Tonto.

✳

Point *of* Grace

*R*ead Judges 14:10—11. Why was it necessary for Samson to be given friends at his party? Do you think his life would have turned out differently if he had been accountable to a least one person? How might a good friendship enhance your life?

_____

_____

_____

_____

_____

_____

_____

_____

_____

_____

_____

_____

_____

_____

✳

Steady On
Shelley Breen

People ask me all the time if I had been a cheer-leader back in high school. That has got to be the most hilarious thing in the world to me. I am so *not* cheerleader material. I couldn't even do a cartwheel. I guess based on our various album covers they must think I've "got the look."

You know what? Airbrushing can do a lot.

The truth of the matter is I didn't even get invited to my senior prom. Right then I knew I could forget about auditioning for the Dallas Cowboy cheering squad.

When it comes to weight, the image projected of me is not who I really am—at least not on a consis-tent basis. There have been periods of time when I was in great shape. But for the most part, I've been a yo-yo my whole life. I've been chunky. I've been

*

pretty trim. I've been up and down more times than a playground of seesaws.

Like anybody, I hunger for the perfect body. But maintaining anything close to it has always been a problem for me for one simple reason:

I love to eat.

I love the feeling of satisfaction that comes with food.

That's my hobby right there. I love food. I take pleasure in reading the food reviews. I enjoy sampling all kinds of cooking. My idea of a fun afternoon is going to a Pampered Chef party or taking a cooking class at the Viking Center.

Give me the *Iron Chef* over *Oprah* any day.

The truth is, if I could do anything in life, aside from singing, it would be to own my own restaurant. I truly do love cooking. The fragrant smell of fresh-baked bread. The sizzle of something in the frying pan. The anticipation of sitting down to a nice meal with my husband and daughter.

That might explain why most of my life has been spent in one of three places: I'm either in the middle of a diet, coming out of a diet, or thinking about starting a diet. Count your blessings if God gave you a high metabolism. My metabolism went on vacation about the time I was born.

*

I remember needing to lose a lot of weight after college. As a band, we were traveling and singing and we were about to release our first album. A staff member of our record company called to tell us we were going to do a photo shoot. He wasn't sure how to say this, but he wanted me to know that somebody in a marketing meeting was concerned. This unnamed person wondered who would tell "several of those girls" about the need to lose some weight for the pictures.

I knew exactly which two people that person was talking about because it certainly wasn't Denise or Terry. As you can imagine, the comment was a painful thing to hear. It totally freaked me out.

Sure, I lost a ton of weight.

But the words stung anyway.

Maybe losing weight has never been an issue for you. Maybe you struggle with the memory of hurtful words spoken by an angry parent. Or with sexual temptation. Maybe you have established a pattern of gossip. Or the inability to speak words of affirmation to your spouse or children because of your own insecurities.

Whatever it is that you are working on to overcome, we're all in the same boat . . . without a paddle. Apart from the power of God, we can do nothing.

✳

Absolutely zero.

Apart from him we will fail. We will stray from the goal. The old sinful nature makes me prone to wander. I'm sure you know what I mean. It's difficult to remain steadfast. So often we put our hand to the plow and then look back on our past failures. Our disappointments. Our poor choices.

Jesus already knows this. He even said, "Apart from me you can do nothing" (John 15:5). He wants us to understand that he is the vine and we are the branches. He is the one who enables us to experience life to its fullest. As we remain connected to the vine, we stay rooted in "the One who gives victory to kings" (Ps. 144:10a).

Do you desire to break free from the things holding you back; the temptations which keep you from becoming all you can be in Christ? Do you have faith that he can give you the victory? If not, a great place to start is to pray, "I do believe; help me overcome my unbelief!" (Mark 9:24).

Then, as you step forward in faith, keep in mind, "It is God who arms me with strength and makes my way perfect" (Ps. 18:32). This same God will be your strength, too. Yes, he will "walk with us, steady on."

Now, if you'll excuse me, I'm late for the gym.

✳

Keep *the* Candle Burning

What is one of the greatest challenges you'd like to overcome in your life? Read Hebrews 4:15–16. What picture of Jesus do you see in these verses? One who judges your failings? Or, one who sympathizes with your struggles?

_____

_____

_____

_____

_____

_____

_____

_____

_____

_____

_____

_____

_____

✳

Saving Grace
Terry Jones

Her name was Rachel. Rachel and her family lived in Nashville and attended church every Sunday just like many families you may know. When Rachel turned ten, her parents made an announcement that effectively dropped a bombshell on her world: they were getting a divorce. The aftershock of that announcement sparked a chain reaction of explosive choices in her life.

Over the next several years Rachel went completely wild. She reached for drugs, alcohol, and the whole range of self-destructive behavior the world calls fun to fill up the void left in her soul. Yet inside, she knew she was dying. She got to the point where she hated herself, she hated life, and she didn't want to be here anymore.

She had attempted suicide at least once. But on

*

the verge of attempting again, she poured out her heart to her pastor's wife. She, in turn, knew about a ministry called Mercy Ministries—a home for girls who have gotten themselves in trouble. Whatever the challenge—drugs, alcohol, bulimia, depression, a family crisis, or an out-of-wedlock pregnancy— Mercy Ministries takes in girls like Rachel free of charge and teaches them the Word of God while ministering to them in the area of their specific need.

Rachel checked in the next morning. But the healing didn't happen overnight. For the next year, Rachel experienced the unconditional love and the mercy of God while also receiving much-needed counseling. Layer after layer of her life was transformed by the grace of Jesus. After she graduated, she shared her story from onstage with us to audiences around the country. Rachel is now on staff with Mercy Ministries, a place where the miracles seem endless.

Mercy Ministries is close to our hearts probably because we are girls who, but for the grace of God, could easily be in their situation. We've watched so many girls leave Mercy Ministries as completely new creatures in Christ. I'm talking transformed, as the Scriptures say, washed "white as snow" (Isa. 1:18).

✳

I have to tell you what really touches me about their approach. The girls get new clothes, not hand-me-downs. The rooms in the home are beautifully decorated to make these young ladies feel special. Mercy Ministries wants them to experience the lavish love of God. That's why everything is first-class. They want the girls to know they're not somehow unworthy or less desirable than others of God's love.

Mercy Ministries wants the girls who come to them for assistance to grasp something radical: in the sight of God, they are not "damaged goods." They are not the crumbs left in the bottom of the cereal box. Or the moldy crust at the end of the loaf. Even in their broken condition, Jesus welcomes them with open arms.

In Luke 7, we find Jesus at the dinner table. He was a guest of Simon, an influential Pharisee. In walked a candidate for Mercy Ministries—a prostitute. She spotted Jesus and, taking a place beside his feet, started to cry and "she began to wet his feet with her tears. Then she wiped them with her hair, kissed them and poured perfume on them" (Luke 7:38b).

You've got to catch the radical nature of this scene.

Imagine if you were having dinner in the home of

a well-known, wealthy personality when, out of the blue, an uninvited hooker walked through the front door, fell by your side, poured perfume on your feet, began to kiss your toes, and then wiped your feet with her hair. How would you feel?

Startled? Embarrassed? Panicked? Appalled?

Jesus evidently didn't flinch. He didn't attempt to stop the woman's display of gratitude. That really annoyed the host, who said to himself, "'If this man were a prophet, he would know who is touching him and what kind of woman she is—that she is a sinner'" (Luke 7:39).

Jesus immediately repented of this transgression, right?

Wrong. He could have given in to the peer pressure and said, "You know, Simon, you're right. She's scum. How silly of me to miss that part. Throw her out of the house this instant! I can't believe such a lowlife would be allowed in my presence."

But Jesus didn't.

In fact, he chided the host for failing to provide such basic hospitality as water to wash his feet, as was the custom. Jesus turns to this streetwalker and says the two things she needed the most to hear: "Your sins are forgiven" (v. 48) and "Your faith has saved you; go in peace" (v. 50).

*

That's radical love.

That's Jesus.

And that's why I thank God for Mercy Ministries and their Christ-like example of unconditional love. At the same time, you and I are called to open our arms, too. After all, it's about "sharing life and giving our own away. It's all about serving God, all about saving Grace."

*

Keep *the* Candle Burning

If a prostitute walked into the middle of the Sunday service at your church and sat down in the front row, what kind of reaction do you think she'd get? Why is the radical love of Jesus so difficult to practice?

_____

_____

_____

_____

_____

_____

_____

_____

_____

_____

_____

_____

_____

_____

When the Wind Blows

Denise Jones

My husband worked in the emergency room at a local hospital here in the Nashville area. Weekends were especially crazy. On top of caring for the usual cuts, bruises, broken bones, and accidents, at least once a weekend somebody would walk in announcing they had a message from God . . . or that they *were* God. Sometimes these "prophets" had been picked up off of the streets by the police—for their own safety—because of their delusional state.

I remember one particular weekend, Stu was preparing to leave for the hospital. He looked me in the eyes and said, "Honey, should I keep working in the ER?" I knew what was behind his question. The long hours . . . living in constant crisis mode . . . and the occasional late-night visit from

✳

someone professing to be God. That's a lot of stress to handle.

When he returned home, he had this giant grin on his face. When I asked why the smile, he said, "Guess who came in tonight."

We exchanged a look and then we said it at the same time: "God!"

I guess we had our confirmation.

If you've ever been to a big city, you've no doubt seen a street-corner prophet. When we were in New York, I remember seeing a disheveled older man, wearing a torn shirt, filthy jeans, and scuffed shoes. He shuffled along the sidewalk, raising his arms as he walked. In a thick voice, he proclaimed, "REPENT! Jesus is coming back! REPENT, I say! Before it's too late."

All around him, the crowd of busy shoppers and professional people hustled off to their important destinations, avoiding his gaze. Some moved to the opposite edge of the sidewalk to maximize the distance between them and the transient. A handful of passersby paused with guarded curiosity to watch the prophetic exhibition.

"Repent! While there's still time!"

I know I came away from that encounter with mixed emotions. Why is it we tend to label a person

*

like this man as maybe "crazy," "deranged"—even "unstable"? What is it about his message that makes us uncomfortable?

"Repent! Jesus is coming!"

After all, his message is true. The Bible calls us to repentance. Remember John the Baptist's message? "Repent, for the kingdom of heaven is near" (Matt. 3:2). Likewise, Jesus himself told his disciples to watch and wait for his return, because "you do not know on what day your Lord will come" (Matt. 24:42).

So, why do we turn up our noses, cover our ears, or at the very least feel sorry for the street prophet on the corner? Could it be we've lost sight of something as marvelous as the return of Jesus? Could it be, if we're honest, we really like living here on earth? After all, you and I have so many creature comforts, don't we?

Nice houses.

Nice cars.

Nice clothes.

Nice big-screen home theaters with surround sound.

Nice everything.

And we've gotten used to the potholes, the rust, the squeaky hinges, the graffiti. Somewhere along the

✳

way we've decided that if his return is delayed, that's okay. We're doing pretty good without him, thank you for asking. Having decided his return won't be anytime soon, we've lost something special in the process.

We've lost the sense of *expectancy*. How tragic.

Jesus is coming back. And when he does, he will put an end to all brokenness. As he has said, "I am making everything new!" (Rev. 21:5). He is coming to right the wrongs. To usher in a day, as the song says, "when the lion and the lamb start walking two by two." How can I allow my heart to grow cold and lose sight of that wondrous day?

In Romans 8:22, Paul writes, "We know that the whole creation has been groaning as in the pains of childbirth right up to the present time." Groaning? For what? What do the rocks know that I've missed?

Verse 21 says that "the creation itself will be liberated from its bondage to decay." Wow! Creation— the trees, the rocks, the very soil we walk on—waits with expectation for the day it will be liberated from decay.

It's funny. When I was expecting a baby, I never once forgot I was pregnant. How could I? Every day my body reminded me something marvelous was at

✳

work. I knew at the right time, my baby would come.

And for nine months, everything about me announced to the world I was an expecting mother. The glow on my face and my protruding tummy were hints. So, too, was my constant conversation. I couldn't stop talking about the coming of my child.

What color would his eyes be? Would he have lots of hair? Who would he look like, me or Stu? What color should we paint his room? Is the crib set up? Has the nausea settled down? Did you see the cute little outfit from Aunt so-and-so?

That's how it ought to be as I anticipate the return of the Lord. He is, after all, the Lover of my soul, the one who holds me in his perfect embrace, who has numbered the hairs on my head and who has saved me. This glorious Jesus is coming back.

For me.

For you.

For the prophet on the street corner.

Or even in the ER.

I can hardly wait for the day, as the song says, "When the wind blows, when the sky is torn in two, and the Lord of lords in all His glory, comes for you."

Yes, Lord, come quickly. Even today!

✳

Keep *the* Candle Burning

*R*ead Matthew 25:1—13. Here, Jesus tells the parable of the Ten Virgins. What can you learn about being prepared for the return of the Lord in this illustration?

_____

_____

_____

_____

_____

_____

_____

_____

_____

_____

_____

_____

_____

_____

_____

_____

✳

Wonder of It All
Shelley Breen

B
e honest. Have you ever fallen asleep in church? I sure have. On more than one occasion—typically when a guest speaker fills the pulpit. Try as I may, sometimes sleep gets the better of me and my eyelids head south. Oh, sure, I'll fight it. But I'm convinced there must be some unseen magnetic force pulling my eyes shut. Within seconds, my head rolls to the side.

Sometimes I'm fortunate. I actually catch myself dozing. I'll jerk my head upright and, in case somebody spied my indiscretion, I'll pretend I had been looking at a point of interest on my neighbor's collar.

As the guest pastor drones on, it happens again. This time, the beckoning catnap overpowers me. A touch of moisture appears at the corners of my mouth. Not a full-blown drool, mind you. Just

✳

enough to require a Kleenex. I stretch, check my watch, smile at my husband, and pray for the final hymn.

Years ago, a particularly dry guest speaker addressed our church. I should have brought a copy of *101 Things to Do During a Boring Sermon*. But I didn't. I was in big trouble. The night before, I didn't have the willpower to turn off some sappy TV show. Now I was paying for it. With thirty minutes to go, I slipped a piece of gum out of my purse and into my mouth. I had hopes that the chewing action would stimulate a fresh flow of blood and oxygen to my brain.

You know what? There's no substitute for a good night's sleep. The gum didn't work. I fell asleep. A deep, peaceful rest. You might say it was a mouth-watering experience. I believe it was the jab of my husband's elbow that saved me from total public embarrassment.

Did you know that the Bible recorded an account of a man who fell asleep in church? In Acts 20:9 we read, "Seated in a window was a young man named Eutychus, who was sinking into a deep sleep as Paul talked on and on. When he was sound asleep, he fell to the ground from the third story and was picked up dead."

✳

The fact that this was recorded for our benefit probably means the problem is more widespread than we care to admit. On the surface, it might be a message to pastors to keep the sermon short. But, in my opinion, there's actually a deep spiritual truth in all of this talk about sleeping in church.

I believe we struggle to stay awake because far too often we the Church, the Bride of Christ, have lost sight of the wonder of God. Look how people reacted in Scripture when they stood in the presence of God or when they witnessed his marvelous handiwork.

Take Job. His buddies were sitting around with him questioning the way God was running things. God, in turn, answered Job from a storm. What was Job's reaction? "I am unworthy—how can I reply to you? *I put my hand over my mouth*" (Job 40:4) [emphasis added].

In 2 Samuel 6:14, when the Lord brought the Ark of the Covenant back to Israel, "David . . . *danced before the LORD with all his might* [emphasis added]."

In Luke 5:26, Jesus healed a lame man who got up and walked. "Everyone was amazed and *gave praise to God. They were filled with awe* [emphasis added]."

In John 18:6, when the soldiers came with their swords to arrest Jesus, they asked for some ID.

✳

"When Jesus said, 'I am he,' *they drew back and fell to the ground* [emphasis added]."

In Revelation 1:17, John shares his encounter with the living Christ. "When I saw him, *I fell at his feet as though dead* [emphasis added]."

Are you seeing a pattern here? When these men came before the Lord God, they either covered their mouths, danced, sang praises, were filled with awe, or fell to the ground, dead with fear. Guess what?

Not a single person came into God's presence and yawned.

I stand convicted. I know I need to discover this mighty God afresh. How about you? Has worship on Sunday been more about getting through the formalities than embracing the wonder? As the song says, "Feel the wonder of it all, let your heart and mind receive . . . the love of God, the wonder of it all."

But how? Sunday mornings are so hectic.

The simple act of preparation the night before can help keep Sunday from being such a tiring whirlwind. Why not spend a few minutes laying out the kids' clothes, setting the breakfast table, and switching off the tube early to get a good rest? You and I will have a more meaningful Sunday experience if we get a head start Saturday night.

✳

Why should we go to all the fuss?

Because the Savior wants to speak to me.

Because I long to enter into his presence.

And, unlike Eutychus, I don't want to learn the hard way.

Snooze, you lose.

✳

What are Sunday mornings like in your house? Why is it so difficult to arrive at church early? What role might spiritual warfare play in getting to church on time? Have you ever tried going to bed earlier on Saturday night in order to be well-rested for church?

_____

_____

_____

_____

_____

_____

_____

_____

_____

_____

_____

_____

✳

My God
Heather Payne

There's an old saying, "No pain, no gain." The picture which comes to my mind is that of a marathon runner, one who pushes herself mile after mile until every muscle aches and her lungs burn for air. Exhausted, she wants to throw in the towel. She'd give anything to sit on the sidelines and sip a Snapple.

But she pushes herself, one step at a time, toward the goal. In spite of the fact that her heart is pounding with the intensity of a pack of huskies pulling a sled through deep snow, she gets a second wind. She presses on. She knows if she persists, there's nothing quite like the feeling that comes when crossing the finish line.

No pain, no gain.

In my case, losing more than forty pounds was like

running a marathon. Now, I should say that at 5'9"
I'm a fairly tall person. It was easy for me to carry
around that much extra weight without looking like
the Pillsbury Dough Girl. But I knew I needed to
make some serious changes. Here's what happened.

About five years ago, Shelley announced she was
getting married. She wanted me to be in the wed-
ding, which I wouldn't miss for the world. Right
around that time, Shelley and I bumped into a
mutual friend who had lost a ton of weight on Jenny
Craig. With an eye on the Big Day, we knew we
wanted to look our best. Shelley said, "Hey, I'll do it
if you'll do it, too."

Off we went. After my initial session, I began
some important soul searching. For starters, I wanted
to discover when and why I first began to put on the
weight. While looking at my baby pictures, I
decided it must have been sometime during my
grade school days. Living in the South, I just indulged
in the wonderful but unhealthy style of southern
cooking. I chose to eat.

A lot.

Let's face it, food is so-o good.

Especially those irresistible cheese fries at Outback Steak House.

Raised as I was in a Baptist church, food and

✳

fellowship went hand in glove. We had the fellowship hour between services—with donuts, cookies,
coffee, thank you very much. Fellowship dinners
on Wednesday night. Pancake breakfasts on special
Saturdays. The occasional bake sale after the service.
And did you hear the great news? Pastor announced
the expanded Christmas buffet. That is, after working up a good appetite caroling down the block in
front of the church.

Hmm.

Throughout my junior and senior high school
years, I had a lot of self-confidence because I could
sing and people were attracted to me on that level.
You bet there were times when I wasn't happy with
myself because of my weight. I knew there was a
thin person inside of me, but I chose to enjoy food
rather than submit to discipline.

Closing the photo album, I prayed for strength. I
knew the road stretching out before me was filled
with mini-markets, fast food joints, bad habits, and a
host of delicious temptations. I knew I couldn't do it
alone. For the first time, I threw myself into a place
of accountability—both at the weight loss center
and, more importantly, in the hands of the one who
formed my body.

I'm telling you, I was rigid. I forced myself to

✳

exercise. I drank tons of water until I was sure I had better buy a raft for fear of floating away. I never cheated. And I prayed for the strength and discipline to go the distance. The Lord heard my plea and was there cheering me on to the goal.

About six months later, by the grace of Jesus, I was transformed into a different person. Not just physically. I found that the act of becoming more disciplined carried over into other areas of my life. I learned I need to be a steward over *everything* the Lord has given me; my health, my finances, my emotional well-being, my spirit, and my heart.

I love what Isaiah 43:1 says: "I have called you by name; you are mine." You see, contrary to what the pop culture tells us women, my identity, yes, even my sense of self-worth, should not flow from what I look like at any given moment.

It rests in whose I am.

Boy, did that take the pressure off. This wasn't an exercise in vanity. I was enduring the pain of saying "no" to poor food choices, and "yes" to hard exercise, because I longed to be all I could be *for his glory.* He, in turn, blessed my desire. He gave me the victory over the chains of addiction which enslaved me to poor eating habits for many years.

My heart resonates with the psalmist: "O Lord . . .

✳

you have freed me from my chains" (Ps. 116:16). And Jesus, as the song says, has "broken all the chains and set this captive free."

Our most pressing need is to be freed from the bondage of sin and death, that's a given. Praise him for his finished work on the cross. But in this fallen world, as the writer of Hebrews points out, there are other chains which can "so easily entangle us." Can you think of a few?

Materialism.

Greed.

Lust.

Anger.

Gossip.

Infidelity.

And, for me, the temptation is to dash out, ditch the diet, and indulge in an order of Outback cheese fries. Sometimes perseverance is so difficult. I feel like that marathon runner, burned out and ready to quit. Just when I feel as if I'm running on empty, he always gives me that second wind. "My God has never turned away. He's with me every single day."

And he promises to be there with you, too.

✳

Keep *the* Candle Burning

Is there an area of your life where you know Jesus is not Lord? How might his name be honored if you surrendered fully to his lordship?

_____

_____

_____

_____

_____

_____

_____

_____

_____

_____

_____

_____

_____

_____

_____

_____

*

The Song Is Alive
Terry Jones

I am convinced none of us in Point of Grace would stay in the band just to sing any old song. Who enjoys leaving their families behind for days at a time? Who enjoys being chronically tired? And, if you think flying is a breeze, you haven't tasted airplane food lately. Most cardboard boxes have more flavor.

Not in a million years would I pack my bags every weekend to sing pop songs about love, or just any other songs, for that matter. Life on the road is too tough. No amount of money would have motivated me to work as we have worked the last twelve years. I'd rather stay home and work part-time at the mall selling snow cones.

We make these sacrifices because we're singing about something eternal. The hope of the gospel.

*

And I know if we weren't fully convinced of the power of the gospel to change lives, that it truly is, as the song says, "the living, breathing message of the mercy of God," we'd stop singing in a heartbeat. But we have seen and continue to see that the Word of God *is* living and breathing and alive today.

What's especially interesting is to look back and see what God was doing behind the scenes in each of us while we sang this song. We were on the Steady On tour and, frankly, all of us had been in a spiritually dry place. By God's grace, the Lord started to reawaken our passion for him, one by one.

God used Heather's singleness to stir a hunger in her heart for him. With Denise, he used the book *Experiencing God* (by Henry T. Blackaby) to cause her to go deeper in the Lord. And I know both Shelley and I were deeply impacted by the tragedy of 9/11. It reminded us that evil is very real and we have a calling to rescue those caught in its grip.

By the end of the Steady On tour, God had thoroughly shaken us out of our comfort zones. I'm not sure exactly how to describe it, but it was as if each of us could feel the heartbeat of a fresh calling upon our lives. Little did we know he was at work sowing the seeds for two important changes.

First, as we launched into the Free to Fly tour, we

✳

were convicted to incorporate a simple presentation of the gospel every night. Don't get me wrong. We've always been clear about our faith in Jesus. We just felt we could do a more consistent and concise job. Wow! We've watched many, many people come to Jesus as a result. And, night after night, event sponsors thanked us for taking such a bold stand.

Hmm. And we thought we were just being obedient!

The other direction the Lord was pointing us toward was the launching of the Girls of Grace events for teenaged girls. We sensed a movement of God's spirit in the lives of the next generation and just stepped into the flow of his spirit at work. We were convinced the Lord wanted to raise up a harvest of girls who would stand tall in an oversexed, morally bankrupt culture.

Whenever we hold these events, we see at least fifty girls make a first-time decision for Christ. We also see a hunger to hear God's perspective on fashion, beauty, boys, and, um, boys.

In a way, these Girls of Grace conferences are kind of like a mentoring boot camp. In Titus 2:4–5a, the apostle Paul describes such a program where we, the older women, are to "train the younger women to love their husbands and children, to be self-

✳

controlled and pure." Yes, there are times, usually after a grueling cross-country flight, when I resonate with Peter who, in Luke 18, was making sure Jesus knew how much they had given up to follow him.

In those moments, Jesus, in his boundless love, takes me under his arm, whispers my name, and then says, "I tell you the truth . . . no one who has left home or wife or brothers or parents or children for the sake of the kingdom of God will fail to receive many times as much in this age and, in the age to come, eternal life" (Luke 18:29–30).

How about you?

Is God at work in your heart, taking you deeper in the knowledge of his Son Jesus? Has he been trying to kindle a passion, or pointing you toward a fresh opportunity, or pointing you in a new direction, where he wants you to share Christ? Maybe he's calling you to get involved in your local church or on the mission field or with your neighbor. Maybe.

If you're not sure, why not listen to "the song moving on the wind. Calling us home, drawing us in. It's a wave of love that's melting all resistance . . . it'll change the world around us if we listen."

In the words of Isaiah, "Here am I. Send me!"

✳

How might you use your talents and abilities to be more involved in your church? Have you ever considered going on a short-term mission trip? If not, what's keeping you from venturing out of your comfort zone?

_____

_____

_____

_____

_____

_____

_____

_____

_____

_____

_____

_____

_____

*

Blue Skies
Shelley Breen

The first time the other girls and I heard this song, there were no lyrics. Matt Huesmann and our long-time friend and collaborator, Grant Cunningham, sent the music over to us on a demo tape. The only vocal part was the words "You are blue skies" on the chorus.

Even without lyrics, the melody had this amazing, hopeful feel to it. I remember talking with Grant about the direction we wanted the final lyric to take. We wanted a real straight-ahead ministry song, the kind of message that would minister regardless of the situation. Grant went to work and then faxed back a lyric.

Frankly, it wasn't quite what we were looking for. Don't get me wrong, we're not that picky. Okay, maybe a little. But we really wanted a tune that if you were driving in your car after a particularly awful day at work and you heard the song, it would lift you up. Or, if you were at home and just received really bad news, we wanted the song to comfort you. Because God cares about all of our circumstances.

I explained this direction to him again. He said, "Okay, okay, Shelley, I think I've got it." He submitted something different, but not what we needed. We went back and forth a bunch of times. About the fourth try, Grant nailed it.

As God would have it, about a year after the release of "Blue Skies," we got a phone call. It was right around the Fourth of July holiday. Grant had been rushed to the hospital, where he slipped into a coma. Evidently, Grant had been playing in a league soccer game and, in a freak accident, landed on his head.

Talk about a real shocker.

At the time, my friends and I thought Grant would pull through. And why not? It didn't make sense for God to take home such a talented Christian songwriter in his prime.

Denise, interestingly, had just returned from spending a week of vacation with Stu and their boys, along with Grant, his wife Kristin, and their three boys. Around 11 P.M. on the Friday night after his

✳

accident, Denise felt moved in her spirit to call Kristin. She wanted Kristin to hear the words Grant had written a year earlier because, in a way, it was as if he had penned the song just for her.

Looking back on those hot summer days in July of 2002, we all cried, we prayed, and we waited. We longed for the hand of God to touch Grant and return him to good health. We prayed that Grant would once again experience blue skies. If only God would blow away the clouds. As Job 26:13a says, "By his breath the skies became fair."

Instead, we learned Grant's situation had gone from bad to worse. About that time, Kristin, who was such a rock throughout the whole ordeal, brought her three little boys into Grant's hospital room. Crouching next to them at the bedside, she told them that their daddy was going to be with Jesus soon, and she wanted them to say good-bye for now.

The boys wrapped their little arms around their father's chest. The heart monitor next to his bed marked the remaining seconds of life as each of the boys said, "Good-bye, Daddy."

The Lord in his mercy called Grant home.

Several days later, the funeral was held at a large church in the Nashville area. Kristin had arranged a

✳

collection of family photo albums and picture frames on several tables in the hallway. As I lingered over the albums, I was blown away by his example. Grant was clearly a godly man who loved his wife, his boys, and the Lord . . . with all of his heart.

Literally thousands attended the funeral because so many lives were impacted by this man. I don't know if this will make sense, but for me it was the worst thing I have ever experienced . . . and it was the best thing I've experienced.

It was so tragic.

So unreal.

And yet, so life-changing.

I was reminded of the hope found in 1 Corinthians 15:22, which says, "For as in Adam all die, so in Christ all will be made alive." A couple of verses later, I took comfort in the knowledge that "By his power God raised the Lord from the dead, and he will raise us also" (1 Cor. 6:14).

At the end of the celebration of Grant's life, the ushers came and carried his casket through the middle of the sanctuary to the hearse outside. Kristin and the three boys walked slowly behind.

There wasn't a dry eye in the place.

As this gloriously sad procession passed by me, I found myself thinking, *I want to live my life like that man.*

✳

I also found the words of this song—the words Grant and I spent so much time kicking back and forth—echoing in my heart: "Lord, the sky's still blue for my hope is in You. You're my joy, You're my dream that's still alive."

Praise your name, Jesus, for you are indeed life.

You are grace.

You are blue skies.

*

If you, like Grant, were to suddenly die, what legacy would you leave behind? How would friends and family remember you? How might you live differently today if you knew it was your last day on earth?

_____

_____

_____

_____

_____

_____

_____

_____

_____

_____

_____

_____

_____

_____

_____

_____

*

He Sends His Love

Denise Jones

As you might imagine, I love to sing. It's in my blood. Both sets of my grandparents are gifted singers. That might be why I've never really considered singing to be a job. It's a passion. Frankly, I'm not sure what else I'd do for a musical outlet if I didn't have the opportunity to sing with Point of Grace. For me, singing goes way back. In fact, the first time I can remember singing before an audience was when I was four—or maybe five—years old.

My grandfather was the pastor of a church back in Wichita Falls, Texas. As best I can figure, he heard me singing around the house during one of our family get-togethers, where we always sang for each other, and liked what he heard. I'll never forget how he came to me one afternoon, gave me a big bear hug, looked me in the eyes, and then told me he wanted me to sing in church.

At first, that was a little confusing. I already sang every Sunday with my family. No, he patiently explained, he wanted me to come down to the *front* and sing "Give Me That Old Time Religion" for the rest of the congregation. Me? Wow!

Give the kid a microphone and watch out!

Going back even further, one of the first songs I learned as a child was "Jesus Loves Me." It's funny, but only now, as an adult with kids of my own, have I begun to scratch the surface of what that song really means.

Jesus. Loves. Me.

Why me? What have I done to deserve his love?

I know there may be some who might think, "Well, of course God loves you, Denise. That's so obvious. You've spent years of your life ministering to people around the world. I'm just a housewife stuck at home with three screaming kids. If anyone should be asking the question, it's me."

Hold on a second.

Whether you are a housewife, a business executive, a carpenter, or you work at a mini-market selling newspapers, I've got news for you. *None* of us deserves the love of God. I've come to see in the

✳

Scriptures that we are all sinners, and we're saved by his grace.

God's love isn't based on *what I do* for him.

God's love for me—and for you—is based on *who he is.*

Isn't that wonderful news? When it comes to the precious love of the Father, I can't earn it. I can't buy it. I don't merit it. I don't have to stand on my head, wear special clothes, or have some unique talent. He loves me, period.

Imagine if his love for me *was* based on my performance. What would happen on the days when I sang off-key? Or when my life failed to harmonize? Would he cover his ears and say, "Denise, right now I can't love something so awful"? Of course not!

Look at this little gem in Matthew 3. Jesus was about to be baptized by John the Baptist at the beginning of his earthly ministry. In verse 17 we read, "And a voice from heaven said, 'This is my Son, whom I love; with him I am well pleased.'"

God was speaking from heaven. He wanted the world to know that Jesus, who was probably about age thirty, was his Son with whom he was "well pleased." Here's the amazing part. Remember how I mentioned this occurred at the beginning of Jesus'

✳

earthly ministry? That means Jesus hadn't performed one miracle yet.

He hadn't healed the blind man.

He hadn't walked on water.

He hadn't calmed the storm.

He hadn't told even one parable.

And yet, God said, "This is my Son, *whom I love*" [emphasis added]. Did you catch that? God's love for his Son wasn't based upon what Jesus had done. We, too, are loved by the Father *not* because of what we've done . . . or what we'll do . . . or the number of albums we'll sell . . . or the little old ladies we help across the street.

I confess, it's a mystery.

God loves us because he does.

He even sent Jesus to demonstrate the depth of his love.

In 1 Peter 1:18–19, the apostle Peter underlines what God the Father was willing to pay to liberate us: "For you know that it was not with perishable things such as silver and gold that you were redeemed from the empty way of life handed down to you from your forefathers, but with the precious blood of Christ, a lamb without blemish or defect."

God loves you and me so much, he redeemed us with something precious. The blood of his Son. Let

✳

that sink in. Let his sacrifice of love wash away your doubts, your fears, and your sense of unworthiness. As we sing in this song, "I hope that one day soon you will come to realize you are precious in his eyes."

No matter where you are, or what your circumstances, you are loved. You are cherished. You are highly esteemed. By Jesus. By the Father of life. You are dearly beloved by the Lover of your soul. You are the darling of his eye. As my pastor once said, "He's crazy about you!" So, come as you are and taste of his perfect love.

Jesus can't love you more.

Jesus won't love you less.

And Jesus promises you both.

*

D o you sometimes attempt to earn the love of Jesus? Do you equate the things <u>you do for him</u> with the amount of love <u>you deserve from him</u>? Why is that a trap? Why do we tend to put conditions on this unconditional love?

_____

_____

_____

_____

_____

_____

_____

_____

_____

_____

_____

_____

_____

_____

✳

Praise Forevermore
Heather Payne

When we're in concert, the four of us share the up-front microphone duties—you know, making the comments throughout the evening. Shelley serves as the emcee. She's definitely the funniest one of the bunch. She can say stuff none of us would ever get away with.

Maybe because she's so cute.

Denise and Terry will take turns introducing the songs. And I, as things have worked out, have somehow become the "Scripture Lady"—which is, trust me, way different from the Church Lady on *Saturday Night Live.*

I remember one night before we launched into the Free to Fly tour, the girls and I had made a commitment to give a clear presentation of the gospel in every concert. It came down to a question of who

*

should do the honors. Now, I'm not gonna say the other three huddled behind closed doors planning to gang up on me.

But let me just say it was interesting to note how quickly *everyone* decided *I* should be the one. "After all," Shelley said with her wry little smile, "you *are* married to a pastor." The other girls put their hands on their hips and, in so many words, said, "Heather, don't weasel out of this."

Nice. Talk about being out of my comfort zone.

I'm a singer, not a speaker.

I had the same reaction as Moses did when God tapped him on the shoulder to take Pharaoh a message. Moses said, "O Lord, I have never been eloquent, neither in the past nor since you have spoken to your servant. I am slow of speech and tongue" (Exod. 4:10). Moses made excuses, excuses, and more excuses why he wasn't the right person for the job.

Just like me.

But when I stopped carefully crafting my list of excuses, I thought this would actually be good for me to do. I'm embarrassed to say, the words didn't flow naturally. I had to force myself to sit down and write out what I believed.

Have you done that recently? If not, let me encourage you to give it a try.

For starters, I knew I wanted the emphasis to be God-centered rather than man-centered. Too often we look at the idea of salvation from the perspective of "what's in it for me," "my rights," and "what I deserve if God were fair" and all that nonsense.

The truth is, I deserve hell.

Really? A nice southern girl deserves hell?

Yes, because remember we're looking at this from God's view. God is holy. As King David sang, "Great is the LORD and most worthy of praise; his greatness no one can fathom" (Ps. 145:3). In fact, the angels in heaven attest to his greatness by calling out to one another, "Holy, holy, holy is the Lord Almighty; the whole earth is full of his glory" (Isa. 6:3).

Since he is holy, his standard of perfection creates a dilemma for us. Why? Because we have been tainted with the blemish of sin. The Word says, "for all have sinned and fall short of the glory of God" (Rom. 3:23).

Well, then, what about the popular notion of just trying harder to be a nice person? Paul must have anticipated that question. He writes, "a man is not justified by observing the law, but by faith in Jesus Christ . . . because by observing the law no one will be justified" (Gal. 2:16).

What's more, there's a consequence to our sinful

condition. The Bible says, "For the wages of sin is death, but the gift of God is eternal life in Christ Jesus our Lord" (Rom. 6:23). We are spiritually dead apart from Christ.

To be blunt, acting "nice" ain't gonna fix that.

But here's where the good news begins.

God, in his wisdom, love, and grace made a way whereby he could maintain his holiness, bring about justice, and save the sinner! The apostle Paul writes, "God made him who had no sin to be sin for us, so that in him we might become the righteousness of God" (2 Cor. 5:21).

That's where the liberating invitation of John 3:16 comes in. "For God so loved the world that he gave his one and only Son, that whoever believes in him shall not perish but have eternal life."

Isn't that wonderful news? Because of Jesus, we can turn from our sin, and put on the cloak of his perfect righteousness. He has made a way for you and me.

As I sat at my desk writing out what I believed, I was emboldened by his spirit. He, after all, accomplished the impossible for me. His life, death, and resurrection enables me to enter into life eternal. How could I not share this hope with others? In the words of Paul, "I am not ashamed of the gospel,

✳

because it is the power of God for the salvation of everyone who believes" (Rom. 1:16).

Guess what? The first time I shared this in concert, I was scared to death. Now I actually look forward to sharing Christ with our audiences. I want them to understand that when we die, it's not the end, it's the beginning. The moment we put our faith and trust in the Savior, we are regenerated, we are a new creation, and we step into an awesome inheritance of eternal life.

As the song says, "How could I say thank you for joy and peace so beautiful?" No wonder I love the way Peter expressed his gratitude for what the Lord has done. He writes, "Praise be to the God and Father of our Lord Jesus Christ! In his great mercy he has given us new birth into a living hope through the resurrection of Jesus Christ from the dead, and into an inheritance that can never perish, spoil or fade—kept in heaven for you" (1 Pet. 1:3–4).

The moment you and I accept the finished work of Jesus on our behalf, we, too, can claim that promise; we will be with him for all of eternity and nothing can take that away from us.

That's what we're about.

It's the core of what we do.

It's why we sing.

✳

Point of Grace

Have you ever written out what you believe? Why not take a few moments to express what Jesus has done for you in your own words. What Scriptures come to mind as you put together your testimony?

_____

_____

_____

_____

_____

_____

_____

_____

_____

_____

_____

_____

_____

_____

_____

✳